HEALING THE DIVIDE

Poems of Kindness and Connection

HEALING THE DIVIDE

*Poems
of Kindness
and Connection*

❧

PREFACE BY TED KOOSER
EDITED BY JAMES CREWS

GREEN WRITERS PRESS | *Brattleboro, Vermont*

Printed in the United States

10 9 8 7 6 5 4 3 2

Green Writers Press is a Vermont-based publisher whose mission is
to spread a message of hope and renewal through the words and
images we publish. Thr oughout we will adhere to our commitment to
preserving and protecting the natural resources of the earth. To that
end, a percentage of our proceeds will be donated to environmental
activist groups. Green Writers Press gratefully acknowledges support
from individual donors, friends, and readers to help support the
environment and our publishing initiative.

Giving Voice to Writers & Artists Who Will Make the World a Better Place

Green Writers Press | Brattleboro, Vermont
www.greenwriterspress.com

ISBN: 978-1-7327434-5-8

THE PAPER USED IN THIS PUBLICATION IS PRODUCED BY MILLS COMMITTED
TO RESPONSIBLE AND SUSTAINABLE FORESTRY PRACTICES.

For my husband, Brad Peacock, who teaches me daily what it means to be a kinder and more connected human being.

Your neighbor is your other self dwelling behind a wall. In understanding, all walls shall fall down.

—KAHLIL GIBRAN

CONTENTS

❧

PREFACE

※

UNABASHED ENTHUSIASM is the glue that holds good anthologies together, and the book now in your hands will, as you page through it poem after poem, show you its editor's enthusiasms. What breathes from these pages is kindness and tenderness, qualities especially attractive and necessary at a time when warmth and tolerance and inclusion are rare qualities. "Nothing," wrote Tolstoy, "can make our life, or the lives of other people, more beautiful than perpetual kindness," and here before you is a book of kindness, of multiple kindnesses.

I learned about poetry—what it looked like and how good it could make me feel—from the anthologies used by two of my teachers, one in junior high and one in high school. Of course my classmates and I made fun of those teachers' enthusiasm when their backs were turned, we being too cool for displays of emotion, but what poetry could make me feel stuck with me, and I've been reading poems and trying to write poetry ever since, poems every morning when I get up, poems off and on through the day and into the evening. Poetry has been at the center of my life and my attention for more than sixty years.

In my personal library I have around 350 anthologies, a couple of which I've edited myself. I love them, such an efficient means for finding beautiful and moving poems. The wrecks and fender-benders in nearly every individual poet's books have been pushed off onto the shoulder, leaving only the poems still capable of taking us somewhere, often somewhere familiar but as seen through a windshield, clean and unmarked by even so much as a rock chip.

Every anthology, too, is an argument for something, an act of persuasion, and this one is no exception. It says to us, what if instead of watching the evening news we were to watch a young man take a drink from a running tap, then wipe his cheek with the sleeve of his shirt? Or see described in words and images a woman giving her invalid father a bath, rinsing the thin hair over his sutured skull. Or what if we just throw open the windows and let in the clean light of every one of these poems? At least for those minutes, or so it seems to me, we'd see the world as a richer, more meaningful, a kinder and more tender place.

Enjoy this book as I have, reading it through, then reading it through again, then going back to mark those pages I want to go back to again and again and again. As Robert Frost urged us, "You come too."

TED KOOSER
Garland, Nebraska

INTRODUCTION

❦

I'LL NEVER FORGET that day before Thanksgiving when I had to fight my way through a crowded grocery store to pick up the last few items on my list. Everyone was in a hurry, carts clanging into each other like bumper cars, the air charged with frenzied energy. As I edged through the produce section, looking for a head of lettuce, an older woman nearby ran into a stack of plastic cartons filled with strawberries that spilled across the floor. I looked around for a moment, then knelt down and helped her pick up the strawberries and re-stack the cartons.

She protested at first, said I didn't need to do this, but I could tell she was flustered and grateful not to be alone on the floor anymore. Just as we were about to finish, she held a single, ripe strawberry up to me. "Don't they smell great?" she asked. I said they did as I deeply inhaled and smiled back at her. It was as if, in that brief instant we shared together before going our separate ways, some very real gift was being exchanged between us.

Points of connection like this, whether with strangers or loved ones, might seem more and more rare nowadays, but they are undeniably still occurring. The project of this anthology began as something I needed to do first for myself. Because of the barrage of blame and shame streaming daily from our screens, and because the media seems intent on convincing us all how divided our country has become, I desperately needed to find more stories like these—of people coming together, bridging the gap and healing that so-called divide between us to share instances of kindness and vulnerability. Soon, as I began to show the poems I'd gathered to friends and post them on social media, it dawned on me that a whole anthology of such poems could be a useful reminder that the divide—if it exists at all—exists mostly in our hearts and minds. As the Vietnamese Buddhist monk, Thich Nhat Hanh, has famously said: "We are here to awaken from the illusion of our separateness." It helps to hear stories about how others have awakened, even briefly, from that isolating illusion.

Poetry, with its intimate focus on everyday moments in time, is an ideal medium for uncovering the grace that is always available to us, especially when we choose to take care of each other in whatever ways we can. I have always loved Naomi Shihab Nye's poem, "Shoulders," about a man carrying his sleeping son across a rain-slick street. I think often of her final lines: "We're not going to be able/to live in this world/if we're not willing to do what he's doing/with one another." We need to bring this same compassion into all of our interactions so that we are never again tempted to ignore the suffering of others. We must do the right thing, even when it's uncomfortable, even if we must inconvenience ourselves at times. And we must embrace the worldview of harmony among all forms of life, embedded in the traditional Lakota phrase, "mitakuye oyasin," often translated as "all my relations."

In "Small Kindnesses," Danusha Lameris illustrates that, though we are "so far from tribe and fire," we are nonetheless still seeking the same exchange of attention from one each other that we have always needed to feel more connected:

Mostly, we don't want to harm each other.
We want to be handed our cup of coffee hot,
and to say thank you to the person handing it. To smile
at them and for them to smile back. For the waitress
to call us honey when she sets down the bowl of clam chowder . . .

Alberto Rios also makes a similar claim in "We Are of a Tribe," when he argues that we all belong here, regardless of artificially imposed borders: "This place requires no passports./The sky will not be fenced."

These poems, and the many others like them by well-known and emerging poets alike, invite us into a closer relationship with ourselves, each other, and the world around us. They ask us to see strangers, partners, family members, pets, and the natural world as worthy of our close attention and kindness. These authors, from all walks of life, and from all over America, prove to us the possibility of creating in our lives what Dr. Martin Luther King called the "beloved community," a place where we see each other as the neighbors we already are. Anyone who approaches these poems with an open mind and heart will find themselves feeling grateful for the seemingly minor moments of blessing that occur every day, often beyond our noticing. Whether standing in line, waiting in traffic, or having lunch at a restaurant, we can always seek out the glimmer of a stranger's smile or the miracle of two souls sharing a very public kiss at the airport, as in Ellen Bass' "Gate C22." We can remember moments of kindness from the past, as Ted Kooser does in "Those Summer Evenings," when he recalls the way his father would "turn on the garden hose, and sprinkle/the honeysuckle bushes," to cool off the house while his family slept. Or like Jane Kenyon in "Otherwise," we can acknowledge the pleasures of the flawless present moment—"the two strong legs, cereal, sweet milk" and "ripe, flawless/peach" that remind us, "It might have been otherwise."

When we focus on the moments of kindness and connection captured in each of the poems gathered here, we become kinder both toward ourselves and others. We feel less alone and find the world a more welcoming place.

James Crews
Shaftsbury, Vermont

HEALING THE DIVIDE

Poems of Kindness and Connection

THE WORD THAT IS A PRAYER

Ellery Akers

One thing you know when you say it:
all over the earth people are saying it with you;
a child blurting it out as the seizures take her,
a woman reciting it on a cot in a hospital.
What if you take a cab through the Tenderloin:
at a street light, a man in a wool cap,
yarn unraveling across his face, knocks at the window;
he says, *Please.*
By the time you hear what he's saying,
the light changes, the cab pulls away,
and you don't go back, though you know
someone just prayed to you the way you pray.
Please: a word so short
it could get lost in the air
as it floats up to God like the feather it is,
knocking and knocking, and finally
falling back to earth as rain,
as pellets of ice, soaking a black branch,
collecting in drains, leaching into the ground,
and you walk in that weather every day.

OUT OF THE MIST

Lahab Assef Al-Jundi

Out of the mist of a million probable worlds,
Out of the dizziness of a long dream,

Like a bee that found its nectar in a field of stones,
Or a poet who heard his heart's music amid cries of war;

The precision was that of divine intervention,
Art born of deeper beauty,

And just like birds find home after a long winter,
And a smile finds its way to a melancholy face,

I found you.

MENDING

David Axelrod

You knelt over the rag rug
my grandmother wove
from the clothes she wore—

heavy wool skirts
and jackets she sewed
decades ago—

it wasn't a large rug
you mended
with needle and thread,

but you seemed small
at the center of it—
those thick, colorful

braids of tartan,
Donegal, houndstooth,
and tweed, swirling

all around you, opening
a portal already
four lifetimes deep—

you laughed, looped
another stitch, tied off
the tailor's knot

and cut the thread with your teeth.

SNOWFLAKE

William Baer

Timing's everything. The vapor rises
high in the sky, tossing to and fro,
then freezes, suddenly, and crystallizes
into a perfect flake of miraculous snow.
For countless miles, drifting east above
the world, whirling about in a swirling free-
for-all, appearing aimless, just like love,
but sensing, seeking out, its destiny.
Falling to where the two young skaters stand,
hand in hand, then flips and dips and whips
itself about to ever-so-gently land,
a miracle, across her unkissed lips:
as he blocks the wind raging from the south,
leaning forward to kiss her lovely mouth.

GATE C22

Ellen Bass

At gate C22 in the Portland airport
a man in a broad-band leather hat kissed
a woman arriving from Orange County.
They kissed and kissed and kissed. Long after
the other passengers clicked the handles of their carry-ons
and wheeled briskly toward short-term parking,
the couple stood there, arms wrapped around each other
like he'd just staggered off the boat at Ellis Island,
like she'd been released at last from ICU, snapped
out of a coma, survived bone cancer, made it down
from Annapurna in only the clothes she was wearing.
Neither of them was young. His beard was gray.
She carried a few extra pounds you could imagine
her saying she had to lose. But they kissed lavish
kisses like the ocean in the early morning,
the way it gathers and swells, sucking
each rock under, swallowing it
again and again. We were all watching–
passengers waiting for the delayed flight
to San Jose, the stewardesses, the pilots,
the aproned woman icing Cinnabons, the man selling
sunglasses. We couldn't look away. We could
taste the kisses crushed in our mouths.
But the best part was his face. When he drew back
and looked at her, his smile soft with wonder, almost
as though he were a mother still open from giving birth,
as your mother must have looked at you, no matter
what happened after–if she beat you or left you or
you're lonely now–you once lay there, the vernix

not yet wiped off, and someone gazed at you
as if you were the first sunrise seen from the Earth.
The whole wing of the airport hushed,
all of us trying to slip into that woman's middle-aged body,
her plaid Bermuda shorts, sleeveless blouse, glasses,
little gold hoop earrings, tilting our heads up.

SWIMMING IN THE RAIN

Chana Bloch

Swaddled and sleeved in water,
I dive to the rocky bottom and rise
as the first drops of sky

find the ocean. The waters above
meet the waters below,
the sweet and the salt,

and I'm swimming back to the beginning.
The forecasts were wrong.
Half the sky is dark

but it keeps changing. Half the stories
I used to believe are false. Thank God
I've got the good sense at last

not to come in out of the rain.
The waves open
to take in the rain, and sunlight

falls from the clouds
onto the face of the deep as it did
on the first day

before the dividing began.

MY DAUGHTER'S HAIR

Megan Buchanan

I haven't yet been able to find words—
a sentence for what happens when I brush
my daughter's hair and divide into thirds
enough hair for a family of four
(one barber said, the rare one I trusted).
Honeycomb-colored braid, she's out the door
for school (green coat, pink backpack), and rushing
right on time, little Virgo, to the bus.

One-woman-show with harmonies, alone—
amazed, bowed down (deep inhale) O the joy
contained in waves on waves: a shimmering song
my daughter's hair sings as she floats
each afternoon high up into a tree.
Against the clouds she climbs, far beyond me.

BLESSING THE BOATS

Lucille Clifton

may the tide
that is entering even now
the lip of our understanding
carry you out
beyond the face of fear
may you kiss
the wind then turn from it
certain that it will
love your back   may you
open your eyes to water
water waving forever
and may you in your innocence
sail through this to that

REVISIT

Carol Cone

What do you see when
your baby comes home at fifty?
Do you remember the child
who couldn't sleep a single night
for two endless years
who wouldn't eat most foods
who pushed your hugs away
who gave kisses to no one?

Slowly, the years passed without
a hug, a visit, a Christmas card, yet
whatever brought the epiphany—
his father's death, a mid-life crisis
or realization that half a life
had passed him by, much too fast—

he came home at fifty,
erasing years of separation.
Just a visit, an experiment,
still prickly but ready to talk,
to reach out an inch or two
perhaps to build a fragile bridge
across those missing years.

TELLING MY FATHER

James Crews

I found him on the porch that morning,
sipping cold coffee, watching a crow
dip down from the power line, into the pile
of black bags stuffed in the dumpster
where he pecked and snagged a can tab,
then carried it off, clamped in his beak
like the key to a room only he knew about.
My father turned to me then, taking in
the reek of my smoke, traces of last night's
eyeliner I decided not to wipe off this time.
Out late was all he said. And then smiled,
rubbing the small of my back through the robe
for a while, before heading inside, letting
the storm door click softly shut behind him.
Later, when I stepped into the kitchen again,
I saw it waiting there on the table: a glass
of orange juice he had poured for me and left
sweating in a patch of sunlight so bright
I couldn't touch it at first.

LISTEN,

Barbara Crooker

I want to tell you something. This morning
is bright after all the steady rain, and every iris,
peony, rose, opens its mouth, rejoicing. I want to say,
wake up, open your eyes, there's a snow-covered road
ahead, a field of blankness, a sheet of paper, an empty screen.
Even the smallest insects are singing, vibrating their entire bodies,
tiny violins of longing and desire. We were made for song.
I can't tell you what prayer is, but I can take the breath
of the meadow into my mouth, and I can release it for the leaves'
green need. I want to tell you your life is a blue coal, a slice
of orange in the mouth, cut hay in the nostrils. The cardinals'
red song dances in your blood.   Look, every month the moon
blossoms into a peony, then shrinks to a sliver of garlic.
And then it blooms again.

GLITTER

Dede Cummings

The child asks me to remember the code name,
glitter, that she will use in case she gets abducted,

in the worst possible scenario; but I see that
the mother stands by proudly, beaming at me,

her crossed arms bounce up and down, to ward off
the chill of the September day in Vermont. She sighs

and knows that I know her cancer has spread, and is
all sealed up inside her like a bruised apple, hardened and sore.

I repeat the code name, *glitter.* The child looks up at me—
the tilt of her head by the horse farm manure pile is just

slightly inclined—sizing me up: respected neighbor,
confidant or predator, teacher and slow learner,

fellow apple picker and horse stall-mucker,
snow-shoer, future pallbearer. She knows, too.

I lean toward the right to match her incline—
we make a good pair with equally rowdy dogs

dancing by our sides: and the child asks me,
again, to remember her code name. I do.

IN MEMORIAM

Leo Dangel

In the early afternoon my mother
was doing the dishes. I climbed
onto the kitchen table, I suppose
to play, and fell asleep there.
I was drowsy and awake, though,
as she lifted me up, carried me
on her arms into the living room,
and placed me on the davenport,
but I pretended to be asleep
the whole time, enjoying the luxury—
I was too big for such a privilege
and just old enough to form
my only memory of her carrying me.
She's still moving me to a softer place.

THE LAST TIME MY MOTHER LAY DOWN WITH MY FATHER

Todd Davis

How did he touch my mother's body
once he knew he was dying? Woods white
with Juneberry and the question of how
to kiss the perishing world, where to place
his arms and accept the gentle washing
of the flesh. With her breast in hand
did he forgive with some semblance
of joy the final bit of fragrance
in the passing hour, the overwhelming
sweetness of multiflora rose, and the press
of her skin against his?

The body's cartography is what we're given:
flesh sloughing into lines and folds, the contours
of its map-making. When at last he died,
summer's heat banking against the windows,
she'd been singing to him, her face near to his,
and because none of us wanted it to end,
we helped her climb into bed next to him
where she lifted his hand to her chest
and closed her eyes.

APPARITION

Mark Doty

I'm carrying an orange plastic bucket of compost
down from the top of the garden—sweet dark,

fibrous rot, promising—when the light changes
as if someone's flipped a switch that does

what? Reverses the day. Leaves chorusing,
dizzy. And then my mother says

—she's been gone more than thirty years,
not her voice, the voice of her in me—

You've got to forgive me. I'm choke and sputter
in the wild daylight, speechless to that:

maybe I'm really crazy now, but I believe
in the backwards morning I am my mother's son,

we are at last equally in love
with intoxication, I am unregenerate,

the trees are on fire, fifty-eight years of lost bells.
I drop my basket and stand struck

in the iron-mouth afternoon. She says
I never meant to harm you. Then

the young dog barks, down by the front gate,
he's probably gotten out, and she says,

calmly, clearly, *Go take care of your baby.*

PASTORAL

Rita Dove

Like an otter, but warm,
she latched onto the shadowy tip
and I watched, diminished
by those amazing gulps. Finished
she let her head loll, eyes
unfocused and large: milk-drunk.

I liked afterwards best, lying
outside on a quilt, her new skin
spread out like meringue. I felt then
what a young man must feel
with his first love asleep on his breast:
desire, and the freedom to imagine it.

THEY DANCE THROUGH GRANELLI'S

Pat Hemphill Emile

He finds her near the stack
of green plastic baskets waiting to be filled
and circles her waist with his left arm,
entwines her fingers in his, pulls her toward him,
Muzak from the ceiling shedding a flashy Salsa,
and as they begin to move, she lets
her head fall back, fine hair swinging
a beat behind as they follow
their own music—a waltz—past the peaches
bursting with ripeness in their wicker baskets,
the prawns curled into each other
behind cold glass, a woman in a turquoise sari,
her eyes averted. They twirl twice
before the imported cheeses, fresh mozzarella
in its milky liquid, goat cheese sent down
from some green mountain, then glide past
ranks of breads, seeds spread across brown crusts,
bottles of red wine nested together on their sides.
He reaches behind her, slides a bouquet
of cut flowers from a galvanized bucket, tosses
a twenty to the teenaged boy leaning
on the wooden counter, and they whirl
out the door, the blue sky a sudden surprise.

FUND DRIVE

Terri Kirby Erickson

She could be a Norman Rockwell painting,
the small girl on my front porch with her eager
face, her wind-burned cheeks red as cherries.
Her father waits by the curb, ready to rescue
his child should danger threaten, his shadow
reaching halfway across the yard. I take the
booklet from the girl's outstretched hand,
peruse the color photos of candy bars and
caramel-coated popcorn, pretend to read it.
I have no use for what she's selling, but I
can count the freckles on her nose, the scars
like fat worms on knobby knees that ought
to be covered on a cold day like this, when
the wind is blowing and the trees are losing
their grip on the last of their leaves. I'll take
two of these and one of those, I say, pointing,
thinking I won't eat them, but I probably will.
It's worth the coming calories to see her joy,
how hard she works to spell my name right,
taking down my information. Then she turns
and gives a thumbs-up sign to her father, who
grins like an outfielder to whom the ball has
finally come—his heart like a glove, opening.

LOVE POEM

Alan Feldman

The sail is so vast when it's laid out on the driveway.
I stake it with a screwdriver through the shackle
at the tack to stretch it smooth,
pulling on the head and clew. Now it's smooth
as a night's worth of new snow.

My wife, my partner, has been torn from her busy day.
We face each other across the sail's foot
and with my right hand and her left hand
(I'm right handed, she's left handed)
we pull an arm's length of the sail
down over itself, then do this again,
keeping my left hand, and her right hand, towards the foot.

Each fold is easier since the sail grows narrower
near the top. Then we fold towards each other
and I wrap my arms around it, while she holds the bag's
    mouth open,
the gray bag that will cover it through the winter.
Then I thank her. And the driveway is visible again
as it is in spring, when all the snow has melted.

WINTER SUN

Molly Fisk

How valuable it is in these short days,
threading through empty maple branches,
the lacy-needled sugar pines.
Its glint off sheets of ice tells the story
of Death's brightness, her bitter cold.
We can make do with so little, just the hint
of warmth, the slanted light.
The way we stand there, soaking in it,
mittened fingers reaching.
And how carefully we gather what we can
to offer later, in darkness, one body to another.

ABLUTION

Amy Fleury

Because one must be naked to get clean,
my dad shrugs out of his pajama shirt,
steps from his boxers and into the tub
as I brace him, whose long illness
has made him shed modesty too.
Seated on the plastic bench, he holds
the soap like a caught fish in his lap,
waiting for me to test the water's heat
on my wrist before turning the nozzle
toward his pale skin. He leans over
to be doused, then hands me the soap
so I might scrub his shoulders and neck,
suds sluicing from spine to buttock cleft.
Like a child he wants a washcloth
to cover his eyes while I lather
a palmful of pearlescent shampoo
into his craniotomy-scarred scalp
and then rinse clear whatever soft hair
is left. Our voices echo in the spray
and steam of this room where once,
long ago, he knelt at the tub's edge
to pour cups of bathwater over my head.
He reminds me to wash behind his ears,
and when he judges himself to be clean,
I turn off the tap. He grips the safety bar,
steadies himself, and stands. Turning to me,
his body is dripping and frail and pink.
And although I am nearly forty,
he has this one last thing to teach me.
I hold open the towel to receive him.

NEONATAL ICU PRAYER

Laura Foley

Let us be gentle
as we tend you,
let us hear
the mechanical whirrs
and hums you do,
feel the vibrations
of our coming and going.
Let us not walk
briskly by, but abide,
breathing in unison,
close our eyes,
or open them wide
as you do—smallest
and most trusting—
of all of us needing care.
Last week,
my first grandchild
healed here.
May the same be true
for all of you,
our tiniest kin,
in sheltering globes.

SQUIRREL, RESCUE

Patricia Fontaine

Grey squirrels have
systematically disassembled
the suet feeders, one completely
gone, another with its green
metallic chain inexplicably
uncoupled. So I fixed it,
slid in a fresh cake of suet.

When I returned at noon
one of the greys dangled,
hind ankle wedged hard
in the notch of the feeder.
On went heavy gloves,
a red wool jacket, boots.

"I'm here to help you," I said.
It replied a gravelly hiss.
I reached out and pushed up,
squirrel, glove a tangled roil.
Suddenly squirrel high in the air,
twisting cat-like, landing
paws-out on a cedar.

Nearby, my heart was quiet,
a shimmer in the place
where we met,
where the "me"
flickered out for an instant,
rescued from its invisible,
shuttered knowing.

ABEYANCE

Rebecca Foust

letter to my transgender daughter

I made soup tonight, with cabbage, chard
and thyme picked outside our back door.
For this moment the room is warm and light,
and I can presume you safe somewhere.
I know the night lives inside you. I know grave,
sad errors were made, dividing you, and hiding
you from you inside. I know a girl like you
was knifed last week, another set aflame.
I know I lack the words, or all the words I say
are wrong. I know I'll call and you won't answer,
and still I'll call. I want to tell you
you were loved with all I had, recklessly,
and with abandon, loved the way the cabbage
in my garden near-inverts itself, splayed
to catch each last ray of sun. And how
the feeling furling-in only makes the heart
more dense and green. Tonight it seems like
something one could bear.

Guess what, Dad and I finally figured out Pandora,
and after all those years of silence, our old music
fills the air. It fills the air, and somehow, here,
at this instant and for this instant only
—perhaps three bars—what I recall
equals all I feel, and I remember all the words.

AUGUST MORNING

Albert Garcia

It's ripe, the melon
by our sink. Yellow,
bee-bitten, soft, it perfumes
the house too sweetly.
At five I wake, the air
mournful in its quiet.
My wife's eyes swim calmly
under their lids, her mouth and jaw
relaxed, different.
What is happening in the silence
of this house? Curtains
hang heavily from their rods.
Ficus leaves tremble
at my footsteps. Yet
the colors outside are perfect—
orange geranium, blue lobelia.
I wander from room to room
like a man in a museum:
wife, children, books, flowers,
melon. Such still air. Soon
the mid-morning breeze will float in
like tepid water, then hot.
How do I start this day,
I who am unsure
of how my life has happened
or how to proceed
amid this warm and steady sweetness?

A SMALL NEEDFUL FACT

Ross Gay

Is that Eric Garner worked
for some time for the Parks and Rec
Horticultural Department, which means,
perhaps, that with his very large hands,
perhaps, in all likelihood,
he put gently into the earth
some plants which, most likely,
some of them, in all likelihood,
continue to grow, continue
to do what such plants do, like house
and feed small and necessary creatures,
like being pleasant to touch and smell,
like converting sunlight
into food, like making it easier
for us to breathe.

END RESULTS

Alice Wolf Gilborn

His turn for blood work this morning.
A routine test, but no breakfast, not
even coffee. Just twelve degrees—
I offer to walk the dog and after
the long ritual of dressing for frigid
weather, I plunge into the heartless air.
An orange cat crouched in the driveway
shifts its front paws; puffed up jays
squawk in the oak tree. The dog
stops—then sneezes mightily,
putting cat and cold on notice.

When I get back, he's settled in his
favorite chair, newspaper on his lap.
Table's set for one; a pot of water
boiling on the stove awaits its egg,
tea bag sits in a mug, a single slice
of toast is ready to pop. The radio
is off for once, so it's our own voices
we hear, chatter we won't remember
in a room warming with winter sun.
When he leaves, silence descends
like yesterday's snow.

Eating my solitary breakfast,
I think of his small habitual gestures,
the way he has of wanting to nourish
the living: sparrows peck seed he's
spread on the deck, his two feral

cats feed at their bowl, at the table
I'm about to crack a perfect egg.
Sustenance of many years. I wish
him well, I wish him love, food
for our braided lives. I wish
all results positive.

MARRIAGE

Dan Gerber

When you are angry it's your gentle self
I love until that's who you are.
In any case, I can't love this anger any more
than I can warm my heart with ice.
I go on loving your smile
till it finds its way back to your face.

SUMMER MOWING

Jennifer Gray

He has transformed
his Tonka dump truck
into a push mower, using

lumber scraps and duct tape
to construct a handle
on the front end of the dump box.

One brave screw
holds the makeshift
contraption together.

All summer they outline
the edges of these acres,
first Daddy, and then,

behind him
this small echo, each
dodging the same stumps,

pausing to slap a mosquito,
or rest in the shade,
before once again pacing

out into the light,
where first one,
and then the other,

leans forward to guide the mowers
along the bright edges
of this familiar world.

SLEEPING WITH THE CHIHUAHUA

Tami Haaland

In the evening she comes to me
like a child ready for bed.
She slips under covers, curls
into my curves or stretches against
my spine. Some have said they fear
I might crush her, but we're a tender
pair, each aware of the warmth
and the other.

I knew a woman once who kept
an orphaned antelope, let it
roam her kitchen, sleep in her bed,
musky scent and hooves.

This dog looks like a small deer,
poised and silent in the lawn,
but at night, she is a dark body, lean
and long against the lavender cotton
of my summer sleeping. We are bone
and bone, muscle and muscle,
and underneath each surface
a quiet and insistent pulse.

SUMMER KITCHEN

Donald Hall

In June's high light she stood at the sink
With a glass of wine
And listened for the bobolink
And crushed garlic in late sunshine.

I watched her cooking, from my chair.
She pressed her lips
Together, reached for kitchenware,
And tasted sauce from fingertips.

"It's ready now. Come on," she said.
"You light the candle."
We ate, and talked, and went to bed,
And slept. It was a miracle.

REMEMBER

Joy Harjo

Remember the sky that you were born under,
know each of the star's stories.
Remember the moon, know who she is.
Remember the sun's birth at dawn, that is the
strongest point of time. Remember sundown
and the giving away to night.
Remember your birth, how your mother struggled
to give you form and breath. You are evidence of
her life, and her mother's, and hers.
Remember your father. He is your life, also.
Remember the earth whose skin you are:
red earth, black earth, yellow earth, white earth
brown earth, we are earth.
Remember the plants, trees, animal life who all have their
tribes, their families, their histories, too. Talk to them,
listen to them. They are alive poems.
Remember the wind. Remember her voice. She knows the
origin of this universe.
Remember you are all people and all people
are you.
Remember you are this universe and this
universe is you.
Remember all is in motion, is growing, is you.
Remember language comes from this.
Remember the dance language is, that life is.
Remember.

A DRINK OF WATER

Jeffrey Harrison

When my nineteen-year-old son turns on the kitchen tap
and leans down over the sink and tilts his head sideways
to drink directly from the stream of cool water,
I think of my older brother, now almost ten years gone,
who used to do the same thing at that age;

and when he lifts his head back up and, satisfied,
wipes the water dripping from his cheek
with his shirtsleeve, it's the same casual gesture
my brother used to make; and I don't tell him
to use a glass, the way our father told my brother,

because I like remembering my brother
when he was young, decades before anything
went wrong, and I like the way my son
becomes a little more my brother for a moment
through this small habit born of a simple need,

which, natural and unprompted, ties them together
across the bounds of death, and across time ...
as if the clear stream flowed between two worlds
and entered this one through the kitchen faucet,
my son and brother drinking the same water.

WHEN I TAUGHT HER HOW
TO TIE HER SHOES

Penny Harter

A revelation, the student
in high school who didn't know
how to tie her shoes.

I took her into the book-room, knowing
what I needed to teach was perhaps more
important than Shakespeare or grammar,

guided her hands through the looping,
the pulling of the ends. After several
tries, she got it, walked out the door

empowered. How many lessons are like
that—skills never mastered in childhood,
simple tasks ignored, let go for years?

This morning, my head bald from chemotherapy,
my feet farther away than they used to be
as I bend to my own shoes, that student

returns to teach me the meaning of life:
to simply tie the laces and walk out
of myself into this sunny winter day.

KNITTING PATTERN

Margaret Hasse

She took me in hand, taught me
to knit wool from lambs
she raised to sheep.

With my torn jeans and dirty face
I was wild as a barn cat.
She gave me the quiet
of her farmhouse, helped me cast on
into the realm of soft clicking,
elbows moving up and down
like bellows breathing.

I learned the delicate dip and dive
of needles and the patient way
to stockinet, garter, seed.
How not to drop a stitch.

Now a neighbor child
whose mother says can't sit still
comes to me for lessons.
Her feet don't reach the floor
but the scarf grows long
on her needles.

After we finish a session
we go out on the back porch
to bark and yowl, as I did
with my teacher who said:
*Calm down a bit
but don't get prissy.*

PLANTING PEAS

Linda Hasselstrom

It's not spring yet, but I can't
wait anymore. I get the hoe,
pull back the snow from the old
furrows, expose the rich dark earth.
I bare my hand and dole out shriveled peas,
one by one.

I see my grandmother's hand,
doing just this, dropping peas
into gray gumbo that clings like clay.
This moist earth is rich and dark
as chocolate cake.

Her hands cradle
baby chicks; she finds kittens in the loft
and hands them down to me, safe beside
the ladder leading up to darkness.

I miss
her smile, her blue eyes, her biscuits and gravy,
but mostly her hands.
I push a pea into the earth,
feel her hands pushing me back. She'll come in May,
she says, in long straight rows,
dancing in light green dresses.

SOAKING UP SUN

Tom Hennen

Today there is the kind of sunshine old men love, the kind of day when my grandfather would sit on the south side of the wooden corncrib where the sunlight warmed slowly all through the day like a wood stove. One after another dry leaves fell. No painful memories came. Everything was lit by a halo of light. The cornstalks glinted bright as pieces of glass. From the fields and cottonwood grove came the damp smell of mushrooms, of things going back to earth. I sat with my grandfather then. Sheep came up to us as we sat there, their oily wool so warm to my fingers, like a strange and magic snow. My grandfather whittled sweet smelling apple sticks just to get at the scent. His thumb had a permanent groove in it where the back of the knife blade rested. He let me listen to the wind, the wild geese, the soft dialect of sheep, while his own silence taught me every secret thing he knew.

BOWL

Jane Hirshfield

If meat is put into the bowl, meat is eaten.

If rice is put into the bowl, it may be cooked.

If a shoe is put into the bowl,
the leather is chewed and chewed over,
a sentence that cannot be taken in or forgotten.

A day, if a day could feel, must feel like a bowl.
Wars, loves, trucks, betrayals, kindness,
it eats them.

Then the next day comes, spotless and hungry.

The bowl cannot be thrown away.
It cannot be broken.

It is calm, uneclipsable, rindless,
and, big though it seems, fits exactly in two human hands.

Hands with ten fingers,
fifty-four bones,
capacities strange to us almost past measure.
Scented—as the curve of the bowl is—
with cardamom, star anise, long pepper, cinnamon, hyssop.

TO BE HELD

Linda Hogan

To be held
by the light
was what I wanted,
to be a tree drinking the rain,
no longer parched in this hot land.
To be roots in a tunnel growing
but also to be sheltering the inborn leaves
and the green slide of mineral
down the immense distances
into infinite comfort
and the land here, only clay,
still contains and consumes
the thirsty need
the way a tree always shelters the unborn life
waiting for the healing
after the storm
which has been our life.

THE KISS

Marie Howe

When he finally put
his mouth on me—on

my shoulder—the world
shifted a little on the tilted

axis of itself. The minutes
since my brother died

stopped marching ahead like
dumb soldiers and

the stars rested.
His mouth on my shoulder and

then on my throat
and the world started up again

for me,
some machine deep inside it

recalibrating,
all the little wheels

slowly reeling then speeding up,
the massive dawn lifting on the other

side of the turning world.
And when his mouth

pressed against my
mouth, I

opened my mouth
and the world's chord

played at once:
a large, ordinary music rising

from a hand neither one of us could see.

LIFTING MY DAUGHTER

Joseph Hutchison

As I leave for work she holds out her arms, and I
bend to lift her . . . always heavier than I remember,
because in my mind she is still that seedling bough
I used to cradle in one elbow. Her hug is honest,
fierce, forgiving. I think of Oregon's coastal pines,
wind-bent even on quiet days; they've grown in ways
the Pacific breeze has blown them all their lives.
And how will my daughter grow? Last night, I dreamed
of a mid-ocean gale, a howl among writhing waterspouts;
I don't know what it meant, or if it's still distant,
or already here. I know only how I hug my daughter,
my arms grown taut with the thought of that wind.

TAKING A WALK BEFORE MY SON'S 18TH BIRTHDAY
—for E

Mary Elder Jacobsen

Not too far from home, I spotted a painted turtle
toddling along, heading across the dirt road.
I paused there in the hush and just stood still,
so I could watch, and held the dog back on his lead.
When I heard an engine louden along the road,
then rev uphill behind me, I shifted a little,
worried a bit, then moved myself over and waved,
flagging down the sky-blue pickup with its gravelly rumble,
until the driver, with his lowered window, finally slowed
to a stop, his eyebrows raised, looking quizzical.
So I pointed out the small pedestrian in the road
and the old man gave me a nod, cranked his wheel,
and curved around us, leaving behind the steady turtle—
who made it—and me, still mesmerized by a moving shell.

INUKSHUK

Rob Jacques

*Note: On frozen trails of the far north, Inuit people
placed five stones in rough human form as a testament
of endurance and as warm encouragement from those
who had gone before to those who were coming after.*

We were here. We saw sorrow.
Across our hearts, emptiness and cold
pulled hard, as they do in you now,
and we pressed on as you will do.
We did all that possibility will allow
and expect nothing less of you.
We stand guard over accomplishment
and a strong journey through all this.

See in gray desolation how we made
this five-piece thing and left it here,
a stone creation to bring you certainty
in this drear, frozen waste, showing
you and we are keepers of a flame
melting chaos. You and we proclaim.

AFTER DISAPPOINTMENT

Mark Jarman

To lie in your child's bed when she is gone
Is calming as anything I know. To fall
Asleep, her books arranged above your head,
Is to admit that you have never been
So tired, so enchanted by the spell
Of your grown body. To feel small instead
Of blocking out the light, to feel alone,
Not knowing what you should or shouldn't feel,
Is to find out, no matter what you've said
About the cramped escapes and obstacles
You plan and face and have to call the world,
That there remain these places, occupied
By children, yours if lucky, like the girl
Who finds you here and lies down by your side.

CLAIM

Kasey Jueds

Once during that year
when all I wanted
was to be anything other
than what I was,
the dog took my wrist
in her jaws. Not to hurt
or startle, but the way
a wolf might, closing her mouth
over the leg of another
from her pack. Claiming me
like anything else: the round luck
of her supper dish or the bliss
of rabbits, their infinite
grassy cities. Her lips
and teeth circled
and pressed, tireless
pressure of the world
that pushes against you
to see if you're there,
and I could feel myself
inside myself again, muscle
to bone to the slippery
core where I knew
next to nothing
about love. She wrapped
my arm as a woman might wrap
her hand through the loop
of a leash—as if she
were the one holding me
at the edge of a busy street,
instructing me to stay.

BEFORE DAWN IN OCTOBER

Julia Kasdorf

The window frame catches a draft
that smells of dead leaves and wet street,
and I wrap arms around my knees,
look down on these small breasts,
so my spine forms a curve as perfect
as the rim of the moon. I want to tell
the man sleeping curled as a child beside me
that this futon is a raft. The moon
and tiny star we call sun are the parents
who at last approve of us. For once,
we haven't borrowed more than we can return.
Stars above our cement backyard are as sharp
as those that shine far from Brooklyn,
and we are not bound for anything worse
than we can imagine, as long as we turn
on the kitchen lamp and light a flame
under the pot, as long as we sip coffee
from beautiful China-blue cups and love
the steam of the shower and thrusting
our feet into trousers. As long as we walk
down our street in sun that ignites
red leaves on the maple, we will see
faces on the subway and know we may take
our places somewhere among them.

OTHERWISE

Jane Kenyon

I got out of bed
on two strong legs.
It might have been
otherwise. I ate
cereal, sweet
milk, ripe, flawless
peach. It might
have been otherwise.
I took the dog uphill
to the birch wood.
All morning I did
the work I love.

At noon I lay down
with my mate. It might
have been otherwise.
We ate dinner together
at a table with silver
candlesticks. It might
have been otherwise.
I slept in a bed
in a room with paintings
on the walls, and
planned another day
just like this day.
But one day, I know,
it will be otherwise.

YEARS LATER, WASHING DISHES, A VISION

Christine Kitano

Dawn at the kitchen sink, sunrise still
climbing across the California hills,
the jacaranda's shaking: an invisible hand
rocks the yellow porch swing, lifts and unfurls
the tarp awning to startle dozens of house sparrows,
their flight sudden and erratic. Beyond
the loosening leaves, my father, as if returning
from fetching the mail, rises through it all,
the leaves and the mist, his hands (smaller now,
it seems) clutched in front of him, as if holding
a letter only he can see. Water overflows
the open bowl of my hands.

LILY

Ron Koertge

No one would take her when Ruth passed.
As the survivors assessed some antiques,
I kept hearing, "She's old. Somebody
should put her down."

I picked her up instead. Every night I tell her
about the fish who died for her, the ones
in the cheerful aluminum cans.

She lies on my chest to sleep, rising
and falling, rising and falling like a rowboat
fastened to a battered dock by a string.

THOSE SUMMER EVENINGS

Ted Kooser

My father would, with a little squeak
and a shudder in the water pipes,
turn on the garden hose, and sprinkle
the honeysuckle bushes clipped
to window height, so that later,
as we slept atop our rumpled sheets
with windows open to the scritch
of crickets, whatever breeze
might flirt its way between
our house and the neighbors'
would brush across the honeysuckle,
sweet and wet, and keep us cool.

SMALL KINDNESSES

Danusha Laméris

I've been thinking about the way, when you walk
down a crowded aisle, people pull in their legs
to let you by. Or how strangers still say "bless you"
when someone sneezes, a leftover
from the Bubonic plague. "Don't die," we are saying.
And sometimes, when you spill lemons
from your grocery bag, someone else will help you
pick them up. Mostly, we don't want to harm each other.
We want to be handed our cup of coffee hot,
and to say thank you to the person handing it. To smile
at them and for them to smile back. For the waitress
to call us honey when she sets down the bowl of clam chowder,
and for the driver in the red pick-up truck to let us pass.
We have so little of each other, now. So far
from tribe and fire. Only these brief moments of exchange.
What if they are the true dwelling of the holy, these
fleeting temples we make together when we say, "Here,
have my seat," "Go ahead—you first," "I like your hat."

AFTER YOU GET UP EARLY
ON MEMORIAL DAY

Susanna Lang

You take the cats out with you, shut
the door: I have the whole wide bed, all
the covers to fall back asleep in, while you
cut up and sugar the strawberries, grind
the coffee, leave the radio off
so I won't be disturbed. The room is still
dark, rain forecast for the entire day,
other people's family picnics cancelled,
barbecues moved into basements, parades
rerouted to avoid flooded viaducts, the iris
losing petals beside newly cleaned graves,
their mason jars spilt into the saturated ground.
But here is my holiday, this drift back beneath thought
while I lie in the warm impression of your body.

MOTHER'S DAY

Dorianne Laux

I passed through the narrow hills
of my mother's hips one cold morning
and never looked back, until now, clipping
her tough toenails, sitting on the bed's edge
combing out the tuft of hair at the crown
where it ratted up while she slept, her thumbs
locked into her fists, a gesture as old
as she is, her blanched knees fallen together
beneath a blue nightgown. The stroke

took whole pages of words, random years
torn from the calendar, the names of roses
leaning over her driveway: Cadenza,
Great Western, American Beauty. She can't
think, can't drink her morning tea, do her
crossword puzzle in ink. She's afraid
of everything, the sound of the front door
opening, light falling through the blinds—
pulls her legs up so the bright bars
won't touch her feet. I help her
with the buttons on her sweater. She looks
hard at me and says the word sleeve.
Exactly, I tell her and her face relaxes
for the first time in days. I lie down

next to her on the flowered sheets and tell her
a story about the day she was born, head
first into a hard world: the Great Depression,

shanties, Hoovervilles, railroads and unions.
I tell her about Amelia Earhart and she asks

Air? and points to the ceiling. Asks Heart?
and points to her chest. Yes, I say. I sing
Cole Porter songs. *Brother, Can You Spare
a Dime?* When I recite lines from *Gone
with the Wind* she sits up and says Potatoes!
and I say, Right again. I read her Sandburg,
some Frost, and she closes her eyes. I say yes,
yes, and tuck her in. It's summer. She's tired.
No one knows where she's been.

I ASK MY MOTHER TO SING

Li-Young Lee

She begins, and my grandmother joins her.
Mother and daughter sing like young girls.
If my father were alive, he would play
his accordion and sway like a boat.

I've never been in Peking, or the Summer Palace,
nor stood on the great Stone Boat to watch
the rain begin on Kuen Ming Lake, the picnickers
running away in the grass.

But I love to hear it sung;
how the waterlilies fill with rain until
they overturn, spilling water into water,
then rock back, and fill with more.

Both women have begun to cry.
But neither stops her song.

BREAD

Richard Levine

Each night, in a space he'd make
between waking and purpose,
my grandfather donned his one
suit, in our still dark house, and drove
through Brooklyn's deserted streets
following trolley tracks to the bakery.

There he'd change into white
linen work clothes and cap,
and in the absence of women,
his hands were both loving, well
into dawn and throughout the day—
kneading, rolling out, shaping

each astonishing moment
of yeasty predictability
in that windowless world lit
by slightly swaying naked bulbs,
where the shadows staggered, woozy
with the aromatic warmth of the work.

Then, the suit and drive, again.
At our table, graced by a loaf
that steamed when we sliced it,
softened the butter and leavened
the very air we'd breathe,
he'd count us blessed.

THE HUNDRED NAMES OF LOVE

Annie Lighthart

The children have gone to bed.
We are so tired we could fold ourselves neatly
behind our eyes and sleep mid-word, sleep standing
warm among the creatures in the barn, lean together
and sleep, forgetting each other completely in the velvet,
the forgiveness of sleep.

Then the one small cry:
one strike of the match-head of sound:
one child's voice:
and the hundred names of love are lit
as we rise and walk down the hall.

One hundred nights we wake like this,
wake out of our nowhere
to kneel by small beds in darkness.
One hundred flowers open in our hands,
a name for love written in each one.

FOR THE LOVE OF AVOCADOS

Diane Lockward

I sent him from home hardly more than a child.
Years later, he came back loving avocados.
In the distant kitchen where he'd flipped burgers
and tossed salads, he'd mastered how to prepare

the pear-shaped fruit. He took a knife and plied
his way into the thick skin with a bravado
and gentleness I'd never seen in him. He nudged
the halves apart, grabbed a teaspoon and carefully

eased out the heart, holding it as if it were fragile.
He took one half, then the other of the armadillo-
hided fruit and slid his spoon where flesh edged
against skin, working it under and around, sparing

the edible pulp. An artist working at an easel,
he filled the center holes with chopped tomatoes.
The broken pieces, made whole again, merged
into two reconstructed hearts, a delicate and rare

surgery. My boy who'd gone away angry and wild
had somehow learned how to unclose
what had once been shut tight, how to urge
out the stony heart and handle it with care.

Beneath the rind he'd grown as tender and mild
as that avocado, its rubies nestled in peridot,
our forks slipping into the buttery texture
of unfamiliar joy, two halves of what we shared.

I CONFESS

Alison Luterman

I stalked her
in the grocery store: her crown
of snowy braids held in place by a great silver clip,
her erect bearing, radiating tenderness,
the way she placed yogurt and avocados in her basket,
beaming peace like the North Star.
I wanted to ask "What aisle did you find
your serenity in, do you know
how to be married for fifty years, or how to live alone,
excuse me for interrupting, but you seem to possess
some knowledge that makes the earth burn and turn on its axis—"
but we don't request such things from strangers
nowadays. So I said, "I love your hair."

WAVING GOODBYE

Wesley McNair

Why, when we say goodbye
at the end of an evening, do we deny
we are saying it at all, as in We'll
be seeing you or I'll call or Stop in,
somebody's always at home? Meanwhile, our friends,
telling us the same things, go on disappearing
beyond the porch light into the space
which except for a moment here or there
is always between us, no matter what we do.
Waving goodbye, of course, is what happens
when the space gets too large
for words – a gesture so innocent
and lonely, it could make a person weep
for days. Think of the hundreds of unknown
voyagers in the old, fluttering newsreel
patting and stroking the growing distance
between their nameless ship and the port
they are leaving, as if to promise I'll always
remember, and just as urgently, Always
remember me. Is it loneliness too
that makes the neighbor down the road lift two
fingers up from his steering wheel as he passes
day after day on his way to work in the hello
that turns into goodbye? What can our own raised
fingers do for him, locked in his masculine
purposes and speeding away inside the glass?
How can our waving wipe away the reflex
so deep in the woman next door to smile
and wave on her way into her house with the mail,

we'll never know if she is happy
or sad or lost? It can't. Yet in that moment
before she and all the others and we ourselves
turn back to our separate lives, how
extraordinary it is that we make this small flag
with our hands to show the closeness we wish for
in spite of what pulls us apart again
and again: the porch light snapping off,
the car picking its way down the road through the dark.

TO PAULA IN LATE SPRING

W.S. Merwin

Let me imagine that we will come again
when we want to and it will be spring
we will be no older than we ever were
the worn griefs will have eased like the early cloud
through which the morning slowly comes to itself
and the ancient defenses against the dead
will be done with and left to the dead at last
the light will be as it is now in the garden
that we have made here these years together
of our long evenings and astonishment

LOVE PIRATES

Joseph Millar

I follow with my mouth the small wing of muscle
under your shoulder, lean over your back, breathing
into your hair and thinking of nothing. I want
to lie down with you under the sails of a wooden sloop
and drift away from all of it, our two cars rusting
in the parking lot, our families whining like tame geese
at feeding time, and all the bosses of the earth
cursing the traffic in the morning haze.

They will telephone each other from their sofas
and glass desks, with no idea where we could be,
unable to picture the dark throat
of the saxophone playing upriver, or the fire
we gather between us on this fantail of dusty light,
having stolen a truckload of roses
and thrown them into the sea.

WINTER POEM

Frederick Morgan

We made love on a winter afternoon
and when we woke, hours had turned and changed,
the moon was shining, and the earth was new.
The city, with its lines and squares, was gone:
our room had placed itself on a small hill
surrounded by dark woods frosted with snow
and meadows where the flawless drifts lay deep.
No men there—some small animals all fur
stared gently at us with soft-shining eyes
as we stared back through the chill frosty panes.
Absolute cold gave us our warmth that night,
we held hands in the pure throes of delight,
the air we breathed was washed clean by the snow.

ON BEING HERE

Travis Mossotti

Let's move out to the twin rockers
on the porch. I'll give you the one
facing west, and we can watch together
the yellow lab as he trots down the street;
no longer rambunctiously lean, he wears
the solid form that old, well-fed dogs possess.

We are but minor rockings to him, somewhere
in the periphery, barely extant, like any
confident neighborhood stray he keeps
his nose up, his pace steady and fixed,
on his way, perhaps, to a memorable hydrant.
You and I know time is valuable, and a poem

can only give so much, but if you've got
a minute, wait here with me that much.
I promise you any moment now a breeze
will cross over the porch to steal a little
of the stuff that makes us us, and in this way
we'll both be giving ourselves up to the wind.

EVERYDAY GRACE

Stella Nesanovich

It can happen like that:
meeting at the market,
buying tires amid the smell
of rubber, the grating sound
of jack hammers and drills,
anywhere we share stories,
and grace flows between us.

The tire center waiting room
becomes a healing place
as one speaks of her husband's
heart valve replacement, bedsores
from complications. A man
speaks of multiple surgeries,
notes his false appearance
as strong and healthy.

I share my sister's death
from breast cancer, her
youngest only seven.
A woman rises, gives
her name, Mrs. Henry,
then takes my hand.
Suddenly an ordinary day
becomes holy ground.

SHOULDERS

Naomi Shihab Nye

A man crosses the street in rain,
stepping gently, looking two times north and south,
because his son is asleep on his shoulder.

No car must splash him.
No car drive too near to his shadow.

This man carries the world's most sensitive cargo
but he's not marked.
Nowhere does his jacket say FRAGILE,
HANDLE WITH CARE.

His ears fill up with breathing.
He hears the hum of a boy's dream
deep inside him.

We're not going to be able
to live in this world
if we're not willing to do what he's doing
with one another.

The road will only be wide.
The rain will never stop falling.

NAMING THE WAVES

Alison Prine

Above the harbor these clouds refuse to be described
except in the language with which they describe themselves.
I stand here in the morning stillness.

Which is of course not a stillness,
the sky spreading open in the East with amber light
while drifting away to the West.

Here I can sense how the world
spins us precisely in its undetectable turn
somehow both towards and away.

The blue of the harbor holds
the sky in its calm gaze.
This is a love poem, be patient.

Between you and me nothing leaves,
everything gathers.
I will name for you each wave rolling up on the harbor sand:

this is the first breath of sleep
this the cloth of your mother's dress
this the cadence of our long conversation

I want to show you how everything
on this harbor has been broken:
shells, glass, rust, bones and rock—

Crushed into this expanse of glittering sand,
immune to ruin, now rocking
in the slow exhale of the tide.

WE ARE OF A TRIBE

Alberto Ríos

We plant seeds in the ground
And dreams in the sky,

Hoping that, someday, the roots of one
Will meet the upstretched limbs of the other.

It has not happened yet. Still,
Together, we nod unafraid of strangers.

Inside us, we know something about each other:
We are all members of the secret tribe of eyes

Looking upward,
Even as we stand on uncertain ground.

Up there, the dream is indifferent to time,
Impervious to borders, to fences, to reservations.

This sky is our greater home.
It is the place and the feeling we have in common.

This place requires no passport.
The sky will not be fenced.

Traveler, look up. Stay awhile.
Know that you always have a home here.

SUNDAY MORNING EARLY

David Romtvedt

My daughter and I paddle red kayaks
across the lake. Pulling hard,
we slip through the water.
Far from either shore,
my daughter is a young woman
and suddenly everything is a metaphor
for how short a time we are granted:

the red boats on the blue black water,
the russet and gold of late summer's grasses,
the empty sky. We stop and listen to the stillness.
I say, "It's Sunday, and here we are
in the church of the out of doors,"
then wish I'd kept quiet. That's the trick in life—
learning to leave well enough alone.
Our boats drift to where the chirring
of grasshoppers reaches us from the rocky hills.
A clap of thunder. I want to say something truer
than *I love you*. I want my daughter to know that,
through her, I live a life that was closed to me.
I paddle up, lean out, and touch her hand.
I start to speak then stop.

FOR MY DAUGHTER

Marjorie Saiser

When they laid you on my belly
and cut the cord
and wrapped you and gave you
to my arms, I looked into the face
I already loved. The cheekbones,
the nose, the deep place
the eyes opened to. I thought
then this is the one I must teach,
must shape and nurture.
I was sure I should. How was I
to know you would become
the one to show me
how kindness walks in the world?
Some days the daughter
is the mother,
is the hand that reaches
out over the pond, sprinkling
nourishment on the water.
Some days I am the lucky koi,
rising from below, opening
the circle of my mouth to take it in.

SIGHT

Faith Shearin

Go north a dozen years
on a road overgrown with vines
to find the days after you were born.
Flowers remembered their colors and trees
were frothy and the hospital was

behind us now, its brick indifference
forgotten by our car mirrors. You were
revealed to me: tiny, delicate,
your head smelling of some other world.
Turn right after the circular room

where I kept my books and right again
past the crib where you did not sleep
and you will find the window where
I held you that June morning
when you opened your eyes. They were

blue, tentative, not the deep chocolate
they would later become. You were gazing
into the world: at our walls,
my red cup, my sleepless hair and though
I'm told you could not focus, and you

no longer remember, we were seeing
one another after seasons of darkness.

MOTHER TALKS BACK TO THE MONSTER

Carrie Shipers

Tonight, I dressed my son in astronaut pajamas,
kissed his forehead and tucked him in.
I turned on his night-light and looked for you
in the closet and under the bed. I told him
you were nowhere to be found, but I could smell
your breath, your musty fur. I remember
all your tricks: the jagged shadows on the wall,
click of your claws, the hand that hovered
just above my ankles if I left them exposed.
Since I became a parent I see danger everywhere—
unleashed dogs, sudden fevers, cereal
two days out of date. And even worse
than feeling so much fear is keeping it inside,
trying not to let my love become so tangled
with anxiety my son thinks they're the same.
When he says he's seen your tail or heard
your heavy step, I insist that you aren't real.
Soon he'll feel too old to tell me his bad dreams.
If you get lonely after he's asleep, you can
always come downstairs. I'll be sitting
at the kitchen table with the dishes
I should wash, crumbs I should wipe up.
We can drink hot tea and talk about
the future, how hard it is to be outgrown.

TOKYO, NEAR UENO STATION

Julia Shipley

A man sweeps with vigorous strokes
petals stuck to the street.

A grey sky hovers so close,
it finally touches my face.

Instantly umbrellas float over commuters,
I walk in a current of skirt and suits, *gaijin*.

One face nears. She stops and holds out her umbrella
so insistently I accept,

then try to give it back, but she pulls up her hood
and disappears like a pebble dropped into a puddle.

I kept this umbrella
collapsed, this story in the folded

fan of my tongue until now:
I raise its spokes, its flower-patterned nylon

above a squall of self-loathing, I take cover
in that moment—her wrist still kindling my sleeve.

KINDNESS

Anya Silver

Last week, a nurse pulled a warm blanket
from a magical cave of heated cotton
and laid it on my lap, even wrapping
my feet. She admired my red sandals.
Once, a friend brought me a chicken
she'd roasted and packed with whole lemons.
I ate it with my fingers while it was still warm.
Kindnesses appear, then disappear so quickly
that I forget their brief streaks: they vanish,
while cruelty pearls its durable shell.
Goodness streams like hot water through my hair
and down my skin, and I'm able to live
again with the ache. Love wakens the world.
Kindness is my mother, sending me a yellow dress in the mail
for no reason other than to watch me twirl.

BEATIFIC

Tracy K. Smith

I watch him bob across the intersection,
Squat legs bowed in black sweatpants.

I watch him smile at nobody, at our traffic
Stopped to accommodate his slow going.

His arms churn the air. His comic jog
Carries him nowhere. But it is as if he hears

A voice in our idling engines, calling him
Lithe, Swift, Prince of Creation. Every least leaf

Shivers in the sun, while we sit, bothered,
Late, captive to this thing commanding

Wait for this man. Wait for him.

TRUST

Thomas R. Smith

It's like so many other things in life
to which you must say no or yes.
So you take your car to the new mechanic.
Sometimes the best thing to do is trust.

The package left with the disreputable-looking
clerk, the check gulped by the night deposit,
the envelope passed by dozens of strangers—
all show up at their intended destinations.

The theft that could have happened doesn't.
Wind finally gets where it was going
through the snowy trees, and the river, even
when frozen, arrives at the right place.

And sometimes you sense how faithfully your life
is delivered, even though you can't read the address.

FORECAST

Bruce Snider

Today, I'm taking my father
for more tests, his eyes

failing even as we walk
out into the knee deep drifts.

Like his father before,
he takes two shovels from their hooks,

the particles of his hands
sewn somewhere in mine,

so much of him
silent in me as we walk

the bright hemorrhage of white.
He starts at one end,

I start the other, each scoop
unmaking the snow, which has taken

over porches, stoops, skeletal trees
hedging the road. Soon,

he won't be able to make out the handle
he's gripping. We don't speak,

piling the crude heaps,
first him, then me, the black

grammar of railroad ties
announcing the perimeter.

The weatherman calls for more—
seven inches by nightfall—

but the old Chevy rattles
as I rev the engine,

my father leaning to scrape
the windshield clear of ice

until he's certain I can see.

TWO ARAB MEN

Kim Stafford

Up out of the Metro at Clignancourt
we weave through the seething throng
of old men holding a clutch of sunglasses,
the man with a forearm of ten watches,
another with a festoon of leather purses
in green, purple, brown, and crimson
all crying their wares in voices
bereft of hope—then the gauntlet
of stalls with jeans artistically ripped,
shirts fluttering their flags of fashion,
African masks, digital gizmos,
many offers, few sales, but then
the heart of peace appears when
two men step into the bright halo
of friendship, lean in to touch
head to head, right, then left, then
forehead to forehead, the close ritual
of what truly matters, deep economy
where the only currency is kinship.

THE WAY IT IS

William Stafford

There's a thread you follow. It goes among
things that change. But it doesn't change.
People wonder about what you are pursuing.
You have to explain about the thread.
But it is hard for others to see.
While you hold it you can't get lost.
Tragedies happen; people get hurt
or die; and you suffer and get old.
Nothing you do can stop time's unfolding.
You don't ever let go of the thread.

EMPATH

Heather Swan

We have to consciously study how to be tender
with each other until it becomes a habit.
—AUDRE LORDE

The pistols glinted in the moonlight
pouring through the trees by the bike path
as two men robbed my son and his friend.
One gun pressed into his friend's temple
as he lay face-down on the ground;
the other pointed at my son's chest. He obeyed:
slipped off his backpack, emptied
his pockets, handed the taller man his chapstick
and his phone, which, minutes before,
had sent the message, *On my way,* to me.
He knelt down and turned his back when asked,
as one might before uttering a prayer,
the universal gesture of supplication.
In the grass, damp with dew, he prepared
for the closing of night, the silencing
of tree frogs, but the gunshot never
arrived. Instead the men ordered them
to run away, and so they ran, hearts glad
to be pounding louder than their footsteps
like bass drums at some celebratory parade,
all the way home. Later, telling the story,
he says he imagined as he ran the desperation
of those men—*Not much older than me!* —
that pushed them into a life like that.
Like a rabbit looking up at the hawk
and not seeing talon or beak,
but the soft underside of the wing.

NIGHT FISHING WITH POPPIE

Sam Temple

I remember the reeds jutting skyward
like spears in the hands of marching soldiers.
Below, rank mud squished underfoot
as we crept near to silent as possible.

Crossing rusted strands of barbed wire
we entered private and protected ponds
with ninja stealth. Taking position,
crouched in bramble,
we set out, casting thin lines
delicately into the void.

Slight tremors found my eager fingertips
as insomniac bass felt for treats.
Slimy lips extended and inhaled,
sucking worm and hook deep inside.

My father snapped his fingers twice,
the sound of a job well done,
and I felt his strong hand grip my shoulder
as I looked back to see his toothy grin
shining in the moonlight.

FOR YOU I'LL FLY

Carmen Tafolla

The earth below us shifts
and the joints of houses ache
with hairline fractures that grow
into faultlines on the walls.

The motors burn out
first the fan and then the garbage disposal,
on my way out the door
to job or bank or nursing home.
The only two burners still lighting weakly
on the stovetop flicker at me.

Things fall apart
sometimes people too
as crisis-after-crisis beats us down.
Deaths and Close-to-deaths
Loss and Deeper loss.

You can no longer swallow,
or pronounce.
You reach a hand of bones
to lift my hand to your lips.
Your eyes catch my eyes with kindness,
carry the message as softly as you can
against this harsh sky.

The song you heard playing before I did,
Por Ti Volaré, I recognize.
You sang a million times, before this disease.
I didn't know the English title

was *Time to Say Goodbye.*
You pull a shining smile out of this stiff
Parkinson's mask
and gently
release me

SEWING

Sue Ellen Thompson

The night before my older sister's wedding,
my mother and I sat up late
hand-stitching a little cloud of netting
to the brim of each bridesmaid's hat.

To be alone with her was so rare
I couldn't think of what I had to say.
We worked in silence beneath the chandelier
until it was almost daybreak.

Soon I'd have a room of my own
and she would only be cooking for six.
We drifted among the wreaths we had sewn,
nursing quietly on our fingertips.

That she still had me was a comfort,
I think. And I still had her.

GATHERING

Natasha Trethewey

—for Sugar

Through tall grass, heavy
from rain, my aunt and I wade
into cool fruit trees.

Near us, dragonflies
light on the clothesline, each touch
rippling to the next.

Green-black beetles swarm
the fruit, wings droning motion,
wet figs glistening.

We sigh, click our tongues,
our fingers reaching in, then
plucking what is left.

Under-ripe figs, green,
hard as jewels—these we save,
hold in deep white bowls.

She puts them to light
on the windowsill, tells me
to *wait, learn patience.*

I touch them each day,
watch them turn gold, grow sweet,
and give sweetness back.

I begin to see
our lives are like this—we take
what we need of light.

We glisten, preserve
handpicked days in memory,
our minds' dark pantry.

PRESERVES

Natalia Treviño

After the divorce, the refrigerator became my favorite
place to shelve. Capers, olives, long after they had been opened.
Chocolates waited next to onions. Spinach aged in a twisted bag.

Beveled bottles, heart-strung names, *Alessi, Hill Country,*
Cold Pressed, Organic. The clean empty of this new appliance,
this vacuous light, this space that would hold the sustenance
    for my body.

Asparagus, pine nuts, edible flowers. But grape
tomatoes wrinkled. Golden soup divided.
The rosemary loaf caked-over—

so many compositions lost as the enzymes dissolved —
warm flavors, tender flesh. These ingredients will survive
only so long in the cold, but can still come to life with a flame.

DOWLING GARDENS

Connie Wanek

Three children ran ahead of Grandpa,
and he began to run, too,
before he stumbled. He fell in stages,
a fall in three acts, and all the way down
there was conflict as he fought
the earth. None of the children saw this
simple drama: Man resists
an invisible force, then submits.
The clover received him; grass and a few
late dandelions opened their arms,
and it wasn't so bad, as falls go.
He rolled onto his back.
What's next? he asked the sky.
Three earnest faces appeared above him,
and one looked so much
like her mother, a worried expression,
the eyebrows like small
caterpillars. He laughed. And that
was all the angels needed to hear.

LETTER TO MY HUSBAND FAR AWAY

Gillian Wegener

The house is not empty without you.
It thrums and bumps, the walls relax and sigh.
The water heater dutifully comes on, rumbles
with heat, waiting for your shower to start.
How many times today have I heard
your truck in the driveway, the floor creak
with your step, felt your breath against
the back of my neck. At least that often,
I've turned to tell you something,
or hand you a piece of cheese or plum,
but it's two more days until you return.
It's just me in this room, with this plum,
with this good fortune, with this far-flung love.

WITH YOU

Michelle Wiegers

Summer draws them outside again tonight
while you and I lay our lankiness down,

your long legs pressing against mine,
as our children's voices stream in

through the living room window.
We hardly dare to speak,

not wanting to break apart
these few minutes we are given.

Our breath slows its pace
as the laughter of our little ones

soothes our bodies. Releasing
thoughts of this week, we share

dreams for the coming ones.
The breeze brings in the sweet scent

of grass blending with the sounds
of their splashes, dancing

across our skin, loosening each muscle.
The closeness of our bodies, completed

by their chorus of play
as we exhale another day.

COMPASSION

Miller Williams

Have compassion for everyone you meet
even if they don't want it. What seems conceit,
bad manners or cynicism is always a sign
of things no ears have heard, no eyes have seen.
You do not know what wars are going on
down there where the spirit meets the bone.

ABOUT THE POETS

Ellery Akers is the author of two poetry collections: *Practicing the Truth* (2015), which won the Autumn House Poetry Prize, and *Knocking on the Earth* (1988), which was chosen for the Wesleyan New Poets series. Her work has been featured in former U.S. Poet Laureate Ted Kooser's syndicated newspaper column, *American Life in Poetry* and in the anthology *Intimate Nature: The Bond Between Women and Animals* (1998). She is the author of a children's novel *Sarah's Waterfall: A Healing Story about Sexual Abuse* (2009).

Lahab Assef Al-Jundi was born and raised in Damascus, Syria. He attended The University of Texas in Austin, where he graduated with a degree in Electrical Engineering. Not long after graduation, he discovered his passion for writing and published his first poetry collection, *A Long Way*, in 1985. His latest poetry collection, *No Faith At All*, was published in 2014 by *Pecan Grove Press*. He lives in San Antonio, Texas.

David Axelrod's eighth collection of poems, *The Open Hand*, appeared recently from Lost Horse Press. His second collection of nonfiction, *The Eclipse I Call Father: Essays on Absence* was published by Oregon State University Press in 2019. He is co-director of the low-residency MFA in Creative Writing at Eastern Oregon University, where he has taught since 1988.

William Baer was born in Geneva, New York in 1948. As a writer, editor, translator and professor, Baer has authored and edited fifteen books, among them *The Unfortunates*, which won the T.S. Eliot Prize in 1997, and *Borge and Other Sonnets*, recipient of the X. J. Kennedy Poetry Prize. Baer is the founding editor of *The Formalist*, a literary journal dedicated to Formalist poetry, and serves as a contributing editor of *Measure*. Baer teaches creative writing, cinema and world cultures at the University of Evansville, in Evansville, Indiana, where he lives with his wife and children.

Ellen Bass is a Chancellor of the Academy of American Poets. Her most recent book, *Like a Beggar* (Copper Canyon Press, 2014), was a finalist for The Paterson Poetry Prize, The Publishers Triangle Award, The Milt Kessler Poetry Award, The Lambda Literary Award, and the Northern California Book Award. Previous books include *The Human Line* (Copper Canyon Press, 2007) and *Mules of Love* (BOA Editions, 2002), which won The Lambda Literary Award. She co-edited (with Florence Howe) the first major anthology of women's poetry, *No More Masks!* (Doubleday, 1973) and founded poetry workshops at the Salinas Valley State Prison and the Santa Cruz, CA jails.

Chana Bloch (1940-2017) was a poet, translator, scholar, and teacher. During her lifetime she authored six books of poems and six books of translations of Hebrew poetry both ancient and contemporary. She also authored a critical study on George Herbert. Bloch was professor emerita of English literature and creative writing at Mills College, where she directed the creative writing program.

Megan Buchanan's first full-length collection of poetry, *Clothesline Religion*, was published by Green Writers Press in 2017. Her poems have appeared in *The Sun Magazine*, *make/shift*, *A Woman's Thing*, and numerous anthologies, including *Dream Closet: Meditations on*

Childhood Space and *Roads Taken: Contemporary Vermont Poetry*. Born in California, she's lived for long stretches in Ireland, the mountains of the southwest, and New England. Her work has been supported by the Arizona Commission on the Arts, the Vermont Arts Council, and the Vermont Studio Center. Megan is also a collaborative performer and dancemaker. She is currently an English Language Arts faculty member at The Greenwood School in Putney, Vermont.

Lucille Clifton (1936-2010) was the author of many collections of poetry, including *Blessing the Boats: New and Selected Poems 1988–2000* (BOA Editions, 2000), which won the National Book Award; *Good Woman: Poems and a Memoir 1969-1980* (BOA Editions, 1987), which was nominated for the Pulitzer Prize; and *Two-Headed Woman* (University of Massachusetts Press, 1980), also a Pulitzer Prize nominee as well as the recipient of the University of Massachusetts Press Juniper Prize. Her honors include an Emmy Award from the American Academy of Television Arts and Sciences, a Lannan Literary Award, two fellowships from the National Endowment for the Arts, and the 2007 Ruth Lilly Prize.

Carol Cone is a former teacher and New Yorker with roots in Northern Vermont. Originally a native of Seattle, Washington, she now lives in Dorset, VT and writes with three poetry groups in the area. She has always been passionate about poetry, and her poems have been included in five anthologies, including *Birchsong Vol. I* and *II, Border Lines*, and *Remember This in January.*

James Crews is a regular contributor to *The London Times Literary Supplement*, and his work has appeared in *Ploughshares, Crab Orchard Review,* and *The New Republic,* among other journals. The author of two collections of poetry, *The Book of What Stays* (Prairie Schooner Prize, 2011) and *Telling My Father* (Cowles Prize, 2017), he lives on an organic farm in Shaftsbury, Vermont with his husband, Brad Peacock, and teaches creative writing at SUNY-Albany.

Barbara Crooker is a poetry editor for *Italian-Americana*, and author of eight full-length books; *Some Glad Morning*, Pitt Poetry Series, 2019 is the most recent. Her awards include the

W.B. Yeats Society of New York Award, the Thomas Merton Poetry of the Sacred Award, and three Pennsylvania Council on the Arts Creative Writing Fellowships. Her work appears in a variety of literary journals and anthologies, including *The Chariton Poetry Review, Green Mountains Review, Tar River Poetry Review, Common Wealth: Contemporary Poets on Pennsylvania,* and *The Bedford Introduction to Literature,* and has been read on ABC, the BBC, *Writer's Almanac,* and featured on Ted Kooser's *American Life in Poetry.*

Dede Cummings, author, publisher, poet and advocate for people with Crohn's disease, has also been a book designer for the past 30 years. Cummings is a public radio commentator for Vermont Public Radio and the author of two poetry collections, *To Look Out From,* the winner of the 2016 Homebound Publications Poetry Prize, and *The Meeting Place,* published by Salmon Poetry in 2020. Her work appears in a variety of literary journals and anthologies , including *Connotation Press, Green Mountains Review,* and *Roads Taken: Contemporary Vermont Poetry.* She is the founder and director of Green Writers Press based in southern Vermont.

Leo Dangel (1941-2016) was born and raised in South Dakota and attended colleges in South Dakota, Minnesota, and Kansas. He earned both a BA in social science and an MA in English from Emporia State University. Dangel's collections of poetry include *Keeping Between the Fences* (1981), *Old Man Brunner Country* (1987), *Hogs and Personals* (1992), *Home from the Field*(1997), *Saving Singletrees* (2013), and *The Crow on the Golden Arches* (2004). Dangel taught at Southwest Minnesota State University in Marshall, Minnesota.

Todd Davis is the author of six full-length collections of poetry: *Native Species (2019), Winterkill* (2016), *In the Kingdom of the Ditch* (2013), *The Least of These* (2010), *Some Heaven* (2007), and *Ripe* (2002). Davis's writing has been featured on the radio by Garrison Keillor on *The Writer's Almanac* and by Ted Kooser in his syndicated newspaper column, *American Life in Poetry.* His poems have won the Gwendolyn Brooks Poetry Prize, the Chautauqua Editors Prize, the ForeWord Reviews Book of the Year Bronze

Award, and have been nominated several times for the Pushcart Prize. Davis is a fellow at the Black Earth Institute and teaches environmental studies, creative writing, and American literature at Pennsylvania State University's Altoona College.

Mark Doty is the author of nine books of poetry, including *Deep Lane; Fire to Fire: New and Selected Poems*, which won the 2008 National Book Award; and *My Alexandria*, winner of the *Los Angeles Times* Book Prize, the National Book Critics Circle Award, and the T.S. Eliot Prize in the UK. He is also the author of three memoirs: the *New York Times*-bestselling *Dog Years, Firebird*, and *Heaven's Coast*, as well as a book about craft and criticism, *The Art of Description: World Into Word.* Doty has received two NEA fellowships, Guggenheim and Rockefeller Foundation Fellowships, a Lila Wallace/Readers Digest Award, and the Witter Bynner Prize.

Rita Dove published her first book of poems, *The Yellow House on the Corner*, in 1980. She has followed this work with several other collections, including *Museum* (1983), *Thomas and Beulah* (1986), *Grace Notes* (1989), *Selected Poems* (1993), *Mother Love* (1995), *On the Bus with Rosa Parks* (1999), and *American Smooth* (2004). For *Thomas and Beulah*, Dove won a Pulitzer Prize in 1987 and was only the second African-American poet to win the award at the time. Dove has received fellowships from the National Endowment for the Arts (1978 and 1989), the Guggenheim Foundation (1983-84) and the National Humanities Center (1988-89). In 1993, Dove became Poet Laureate of the United States and Consultant in Poetry at the Library of Congress. She was the youngest person and the first African American to receive this honor.

Pat Hemphill Emile serves as Assistant Editor of *American Life in Poetry*. She also serves as an Editorial Assistant for *Prairie Schooner*. Her poems have appeared in *Hedge Apple* and *Times of Sorrow, Times of Grace: Writing by Women of the Great Plains/High Plains*.

Terri Kirby Erickson is the author of five collections of poetry, including *Thread Count* (2006), *Telling Tales of Dusk* (2009), *In the*

Palms of Angels (2011), *A Lake of Light and Clouds* (2014), and *Becoming the Blue Heron* (2017). Erickson's work has appeared in *American Life in Poetry, Asheville Poetry Review, Atlanta Review, Christian Science Monitor, Journal of the American Medical Association*, and many others. Awards and honors include the Joy Harjo Poetry Prize, Nazim Hikmet Award, *Atlanta Review* International Publication Prize, Nautilus Silver Book Award, the Poetry for Their Freedom Award, and the 2013 Leidig Lectureship in Poetry. She lives with her husband in North Carolina.

Alan Feldman is the author of several collections of poetry, including *The Golden Coin* (2018), winner of the Four Lakes Prize; *Immortality* (2015), winner of the Massachusetts Book Award for Poetry; *A Sail to Great Island* (2004), winner of Pollak Prize for Poetry; and *The Happy Genius* (1978), winner of the annual George Elliston Book Award for the best collection published by a small, U.S. non-profit press. His work has appeared in the *Atlantic Monthly*, the *New Yorker*, and *Kenyon Review*, among many other magazines, and included in *The Best American Poetry* anthology in 2001 and 2011.

Molly Fisk is the author of the poetry collections *The More Difficult Beauty* (2010), *Listening to Winter* (2000), and *Terrain* (1998) as well as a volume of radio essays, *Blow-Drying a Chicken: Observations from a Working Poet* (2013). Her recorded CDs of radio commentary include *Blow-Drying a Chicken* (2008) and *Using Your Turn Signal Promotes World Peace* (2005). Fisk teaches private writing classes online, works as a life coach, and lives in Nevada City, California.

Amy Fleury is the author of *Sympathetic Magic* (Southern Illinois University Press, 2013). Her poetry has appeared in numerous journals and in former U.S. Poet Laureate Ted Kooser's column, *American Life in Poetry*. She lives and teaches in Louisiana.

Laura Foley is the author of six poetry collections, most recently, WTF. *The Glass Tree* won the Foreword Book of the Year Award, Silver, and was a Finalist for the New Hampshire Writer's Project, Outstanding Book of Poetry. Her poems have appeared in journals and magazines, including *Valparaiso Poetry Review, Inquiring Mind, Pulse Magazine, Poetry Nook, Lavender Review, The Mom Egg Review* and in the British *Aesthetica Magazine.* Trained in chaplaincy through the New York Zen Center for Contemplative Care, she volunteers in hospitals and prisons, and is a certified Shri Yoga Instructor. She lives in the woody hills of Pomfret, Vermont with her wife Clara Giménez, and their two dogs.

Patricia Fontaine holds a masters degree in Counseling Psychology and Transformative Language Arts and taught Women's Studies and social justice for the past 20 years. She currently teaches classes using expressive art and writing as a refuge for those living with illness and their caregivers. Patricia survives a medley of cancers, and self-published a book of poems, *Lifting My Shirt: The Cancer Poems.* She lives on the edge of a big lake in Northwestern Vermont with birds, wind, and a grand collection of friends and family.

Rebecca Foust is the Poet Laureate of Marin County, California, and author of the books *Paradise Drive; All That Gorgeous Pitiless* Song; and *God, Seed: Poetry & Art About the Natural World;* as well as the chapbooks, *Dark Card* and *Mom's Canoe.* Recent awards include the 2015 James Hearst Poetry Prize judged by Jane Hirshfield, American Literary Review's 2015 Fiction Prize judged by Garth Greenwell the 2015 Constance Rooke Creative Nonfiction Prize, and fellowships from MacDowell, Sewanee, and the Frost Place.

Albert Garcia is the author of three collections of poetry, *Rainshadow* (Copper Beech Press, 1996), *Skunk Talk* (Bear Starr Press, 2005), and *A Meal Like That* (Brick Road Poetry Press, 2015). His poetry has been published in former U.S. Poet Laureate Ted Kooser's column, *American Life in Poetry,* and on *A Writer's Almanac,* as well as in numerous journals. A former professor and dean at Sacramento Community College, Garcia lives in Wilton, California.

Ross Gay was born in Youngstown, Ohio. He is the author of *Catalog of Unabashed Gratitude* (University of Pittsburgh Press,

2015), winner of the Kingsley Tufts Award and a finalist for the National Book Award and the National Books Critics Circle Award; *Bringing the Shovel Down* (University of Pittsburgh Press, 2011); and *Against Which* (Cavankerry Press, 2006). He earned a BA from Lafayette College, an MFA in Poetry from Sarah Lawrence College, and a PhD in English from Temple University. He teaches at Indiana University.

Dan Gerber is the author of several collections of poetry, including *Particles: New and Selected Poems* (2017), *Sailing through Cassiopeia* (2012) and *A Primer on Parallel Lives* (2007). He lives in the mountains of Central California.

Alice Wolf Gilborn, former editor of Books and Publications at the Adirondack Museum, is the founding editor of the literary magazine *Blueline,* now published by SUNY-Potsdam. Her poetry, essays, and articles have appeared in various anthologies and journals including *Adirondack Life* and the *New York Times*, and her books include a memoir *What Do You Do With a Kinkajou?* (Lippincott) and a poetry chapbook, *Taking Root* (Finishing Line Press). *Out of the Blue,* her *Blueline* essays, won the Best Book of Nonfiction 2013 from the Adirondack Center for Writing. She has lived in Vermont since 1998.

Jennifer Gray spent her childhood roaming the West with her family following the boom-and-bust economy of the oilfield. Her poetry has been featured in the *Lincoln Underground,* and she has taught English at York College in Nebraska, where she makes her home.

Tami Haaland is the author of three poetry collections, *What Does Not Return* (2018), *When We Wake in the Night* (2012), and *Breath in Every Room* (2001), winner of the Nicholas Roerich First Book Award. She earned a BA and MA in English Literature from the University of Montana and an MFA in Creative Writing and Literature from Bennington College. Haaland has offered creative writing workshops in prisons, schools, and community settings and was named Montana's Poet Laureate from August 2013 to October 2015. She is a professor at Montana State University-Billings.

Donald Hall (1928-2018) was the author of over 50 books across numerous genres. He was awarded two Guggenheim fellowships, the Poetry Society of America's Robert Frost Medal, a Lifetime Achievement award from the New Hampshire Writers and Publisher Project, and the Ruth Lilly Prize for Poetry. Hall also served as Poet Laureate of New Hampshire from 1984 to 1989. In December 1993, he and his late wife Jane Kenyon were the subject of an Emmy Award-winning Bill Moyers documentary, *A Life Together*. In 2006, Hall was appointed U.S. Poet Laureate and served for one year. In 2010, he received a National Medal of Arts from President Barack Obama. Hall died on June 23, 2018, at his family's ancestral farm, Eagle Pond, in Wilmot, New Hampshire.

Joy Harjo was born in Tulsa, Oklahoma and is a member of the Mvskoke Nation. Her seven books of poetry, which includes such well-known titles as *How We Became Human: New and Selected Poems*, *The Woman Who Fell From the Sky*, and *She Had Some Horses,* have garnered many awards. These include the New Mexico Governor's Award for Excellence in the Arts, the Lifetime Achievement Award from the Native Writers Circle of the Americas; and the William Carlos Williams Award from the Poetry Society of America. Harjo writes a column, "Comings and Goings," for her tribal newspaper, *The Muscogee Nation News*. She lives in Albuquerque, New Mexico.

Jeffrey Harrison is the author of five full-length books of poetry: The Singing Underneath (1988), selected by James Merrill for the National Poetry Series, Signs of Arrival (1996), Feeding the Fire (2001), Incomplete Knowledge (2006), which was runner-up for the Poets' Prize, and Into Daylight, published in 2014 by Tupelo Press as the winner of the Dorset Prize. A recipient of Guggenheim and NEA Fellowships, he has published poems in *The New Republic, The New Yorker, The Nation, Poetry, The Yale Review, The Hudson Review, American Poetry Review, The Paris Review, Poets of the New Century, The Twentieth Century in Poetry*, and in many other magazines and anthologies. He lives in Massachusetts.

Penny Harter is the author of many poetry books and chapbooks, including *The Resonance Around Us* (Mountains & Rivers Press, 2013) and *The Night Marsh* (WordTech Editions, 2008). Harter has received three fellowships in poetry from the New Jersey State Council on the Arts and a fellowship in teaching writing from the Geraldine R. Dodge Foundation. She also received the Mary Carolyn Davies Memorial Award from the Poetry Society of America, and was named the first recipient of the William O. Douglas Nature Writing Award for her poems in *American Nature Writing 2002*. Harter lives and teaches in New Jersey.

Margaret Hasse is the author of five books of poems: *Stars Above, Stars Below* (1985); *In a Sheep's Eye, Darling* (1993); *Milk and Tides* (2008); *Earth's Appetite* (2013); and *Between Us* (2016). She is a recipient of grants and fellowships from the National Endowment for the Arts, McKnight Foundation, Loft Literary Center's Career Initiative Program, Minnesota State Arts Board, and Jerome Foundation. Her work has been published in other anthologies (such as *Where One Voice Ends, Another Begins: 150 Years of Minnesota Poetry*, and *To Sing Along the Way: Minnesota Women's Voices from Pre-Territorial Day to the Present*), magazines, broadsides, and unusual places such as sidewalks, public art, and in Garrison Keillor's *The Writer's Almanac*. She lives in Minnesota.

Linda Hasselstrom is a poet, essayist, and working ranch woman. She has received many awards for her writing, including a National Endowment for the Arts fellowship in poetry and a South Dakota Arts Council literature fellowship. Her most recent books are *Gathering from the Grassland* (High Plains Press, 2017), winner of the Sarton Women's Book Award, and *Dakota: Bones, Grass, Sky- -Collected and New Poems* (Spoon River Poetry Press, 2017). She makes her home in South Dakota.

Tom Hennen is the author of six books of poetry, including *Darkness Sticks to Everything: Collected and New Poems* (Copper Canyon Press, 2013), and was born and raised in rural Minnesota. After abandoning college, he married and began work as a letterpress and offset printer. He helped found the Minnesota Writer's

Publishing House, then worked for the Department of Natural Resources wildlife section, and later at the Sand Lake National Wildlife Refuge in South Dakota. Now retired, he lives in Minnesota.

Jane Hirshfield is the author of eight poetry books, including *The Beauty*, long-listed for the 2015 National Book Award and *Come, Thief*, finalist for the National Book Critics Circle Award. Her next collection, *Ledger*, will appear in early 2020. She is also the author of two now-classic books of essays, *Nine Gates* and *Ten Windows*, and editor/co-translator of four books collecting world poets from the past. Honors include fellowships from the Guggenheim and Rockefeller foundations, the National Endowment for the Arts, and The Academy of American Poets; the California Book Award, Poetry Center Book Award, and best book of the year selections from *The Washington Post, San Francisco Chronicle*, and England's *Financial Times*. Hirshfield is the founder of the *Poets For Science* project and chancellor emerita of The Academy of American Poets.

Linda Hogan is the author of several poetry collections, including *Dark. Sweet.: New & Selected Poems* (Coffee House Press, 2014); *Rounding the Human Corners* (Coffee House Press, 2008); *The Book of Medicines* (Coffee House Press, 1993), which received the Colorado Book Award and was a finalist for the National Book Critics Circle Award; and *Seeing Through the Sun* (University of Massachusetts Press, 1985). She currently serves as writer-in-residence for the Chickasaw Nation, and in 2007 she was inducted into the Chickasaw Hall of Fame. Her other honors and awards include fellowships from the National Endowment for the Arts and the Guggenheim Foundation, the Henry David Thoreau Prize for Nature Writing, a Lannan Literary Award for Poetry, and a Lifetime Achievement Award from the Native Writers Circle of the Americas. She lives in Colorado.

Marie Howe worked as a newspaper reporter and teacher before receiving her MFA from Columbia University in 1983. She is the author of *Magdalene* (W. W. Norton, 2017), which was long-listed for the National Book Award; *The Kingdom of Ordinary Time* (W. W. Norton, 2009), which was a finalist for the *Los Angeles Times Book Prize; What the Living Do* (W. W. Norton, 1998); and *The Good Thief* (Persea Books, 1988), which was selected by Margaret Atwood for the 1987 National Poetry Series. Currently, she teaches at New York University and Sarah Lawrence College, and lives in New York City with her daughter.

Joseph Hutchison, Poet Laureate of Colorado (2014-2019), is the author of 19 collections of poems, including *Eyes of the Cuervo/ Ojos Del Crow* (a bilingual edition of his Mexico poems translated by Patricia Herminia), *The World As Is: New & Selected Poems, 1972-2015, Marked Men, Thread of the Real, Bed of Coals* (winner of the Colorado Poetry Award), and the Colorado Governor's Award volume, *Shadow-Light*. He has also translated *Ephemeral*, a collection of flash fictions by Mexican author Miguel Lupián. His poems have appeared in over 100 journals and several anthologies, including New Poets of the American West, and he has co-edited two anthologies, *Malala: Poems for Malala Yousafzai* (all profits benefit the Malala Fund for girls' education worldwide) and *A Song for Occupations: Poems About the American Way of Work*.

Mary Elder Jacobsen's poetry has appeared in *Cold Mountain Review, The Cincinnati Review, The Greensboro Review, GMR Online*, and *Poetry Daily*. She is at work on a first collection of poetry, *Stonechat*, has poetry in the anthology *Birchsong, Vol. II, The Remembered Arts Journal*, and other venues, and is a recent recipient of a Vermont Studio Center residency. She holds an MA from The Writing Seminars at Johns Hopkins University, where she was a Teaching Fellow, and an MFA from UNC-Greensboro. She is co-curator of the annual reading series Words Out Loud, in conjunction with Art at the Kent in Calais, Vermont, where she works as an editor and lives with her family on a hill above a lake in a pocket of wild woods.

Rob Jacques resides on a rural island in Washington State's Puget Sound, and his poetry appears in literary journals, including *Atlanta Review, Prairie Schooner, Amsterdam Quarterly, Poet Lore,*

The Healing Muse, and *Assaracus.* A collection of his poems, *War Poet,* was published by Sibling Rivalry Press in 2017.

Mark Jarman is Centennial Professor of English at Vanderbilt University and the author of ten books of poetry, two books of essays, and a book of essays co-authored with Robert McDowell. He co-edited the anthology *Rebel Angels: 25 Poets of the New Formalism* with David Mason.

Kasey Jueds holds degrees from Harvard, Stanford, and Sarah Lawrence College. Her first collection of poems, *Keeper,* won the Agnes Lynch Starrett Prize and was published by the University of Pittsburgh Press in 2013. Her work has appeared in journals including *The American Poetry Review, Beloit Poetry Journal, Prairie Schooner, Crab Orchard Review, 5AM, Women's Review of Books, Salamander,* and *Manhattan Review.* She works in educational research and lives in Philadelphia.

Julia Kasdorf is the author of the poetry collections *Shale Play: Poems and Photographs from the Fracking Fields* (Penn State University Press, 2018), which includes photographs by Steven Rubin; *Poetry in America* (University of Pittsburgh Press, 2011); *Eve's Striptease* (University of Pittsburgh Press, 1998); and *Sleeping Preacher* (University of Pittsburgh Press, 1992), which received the 1991 Agnes Lynch Starrett Poetry Prize and the Great Lakes Colleges Award for New Writing in 1993. Kasdorf teaches creative writing at Pennsylvania State University.

Jane Kenyon (1947-1995) was an American poet and translator. While a student at the University of Michigan, Kenyon met the poet Donald Hall; though he was more than twenty years her senior, she married him in 1972, and they moved to Eagle Pond Farm, his ancestral home in New Hampshire. Kenyon was New Hampshire's poet laureate when she died in April of 1995 from leukemia. When she died, she was working on editing the now-classic *Otherwise: New and Selected Poems,* which was released posthumously in 1996.

Christine Kitano was born in Los Angeles, CA. Her mother is a first-generation immigrant from Korea, and her father is *nisei* (second-generation) Japanese American. Christine earned an MFA in Creative Writing (poetry) from Syracuse University and a PhD in English and Creative Writing from Texas Tech University. She is an assistant professor at Ithaca College where she teaches creative writing, poetry, and Asian American literature. She is the author of the poetry collections *Sky Country* (BOA Editions) and *Birds of Paradise* (Lynx House).

Ron Koertge teaches at Hamline University in their low-residency MFA program for Children's Writing. He has published widely in such magazines as *Kayak* and *Poetry Now*. Sumac Press issued *The Father Poems* in 1973, which was followed by many more books of poetry including *Fever* (Red Hen Press, 2007), *Indigo* (Red Hen Press, 2009), and *Lies, Knives and Girls in Red Dresses* (Candlewick Press, 2012). Koertge also writes fiction for teenagers, including many novels-in-verse: *The Brimstone Journals, Stoner & Spaz, Strays, Shakespeare Bats Cleanup,* and *Shakespeare Makes the Playoffs.* He lives in South Pasadena, California.

Ted Kooser, 13th United States Poet Laureate (2004-2006), is a retired life insurance executive who lives on an acreage near the village of Garland, Nebraska, with his wife, Kathleen Rutledge. His collection *Delights & Shadows* was awarded the Pulitzer Prize in Poetry in 2005. His poems have appeared in *The Atlantic Monthly, Hudson Review, Antioch Review, Kenyon Review* and dozens of other literary journals. His memoir, *Local Wonders: Seasons in the Bohemian Alps,* a Barnes & Noble Discover finalist in nonfiction, also won the 2002 Friends of American Writers Award and *ForeWord Magazine's* Gold Medal recognition for autobiographical writing. His newest collection, *Kindest Regards: New and Selected Poems,* was published by Copper Canyon Press in 2018.

Danusha Laméris lives in California, where she currently serves as Poet Laureate of Santa Cruz County. She is the author of *Moons of August,* chosen by Naomi Shihab Nye as winner of the Autumn House Press Poetry Prize for 2013. Her work has been published or is forthcoming in: *Best American Poetry, The American Poetry*

Review, The New York Times Magazine, New Letters, Ploughshares, The Gettysburg Review, The SUN, and *Tin House*, among other journals.

Susanna Lang has published original poems, essays and translations from the French, in such journals as *Kalliope, Sport Literate, Southern Poetry Review, Chicago Review, New Directions*, and *Whetstone*, as well as online at the *Red River Review*. Book publications include translations of *Words in Stone* and *The Origin of Language*, both by Yves Bonnefoy.

Dorianne Laux is the author of several collections of poetry, including *What We Carry* (1994), a finalist for the National Book Critics Circle Award; *Smoke* (2000); *Facts about the Moon* (2005), chosen by the poet Ai as winner of the Oregon Book Award and also a finalist for the Lenore Marshall Poetry Prize; *The Book of Men* (2011), which was awarded the Paterson Prize; and *Only As the Day is Long: New and Selected Poems* (2018). She has received fellowships from the Guggenheim Foundation and the National Endowment for the Arts, and has been a Pushcart Prize winner. She lives with her husband, poet Joseph Millar, in North Carolina.

Li-young Lee was born in Djakarta, Indonesia in 1957 to Chinese political exiles. Both of Lee's parents came from powerful Chinese families: Lee's great grandfather was the first president of the Republic of China, and Lee's father had served as personal physician to Mao Zedong. He is the author of The Undressing (W. W. Norton, 2018); *Behind My Eyes* (W. W. Norton, 2008); *Book of My Nights* (BOA Editions, 2001), which won the 2002 William Carlos Williams Award; *The City in Which I Love You* (BOA Editions, 1990), which was the 1990 Lamont Poetry Selection; and *Rose* (BOA Editions, 1986), which won the Delmore Schwartz Memorial Poetry Award. He lives in Chicago, Illinois, with his wife and their two sons.

Richard Levine is the author of the poetry collections *Contiguous States* (Finishing Line Press, 2018) and *Selected Poems* (Future Cycle Press, 2019), as well five chapbooks: *The Cadence of Mercy, A Tide of* *a Hundred Mountains, That Country's Soul, A Language Full of Wars and Songs,* and *Snapshots from a Battle.*

Annie Lighthart is a writer and teacher in Portland, Oregon. She earned an MFA in Poetry from Vermont College of Fine Arts and has taught at Boston College, as a poet in the schools, and with many community groups. Her poems have appeared in *The Greensboro Review, Cimarron Review, CALYX,* and other publications, and she is the author of *Iron String,* published by Airlie Press in 2013.

Diane Lockward is the author of *The Crafty Poet II: A Portable Workshop* (Terrapin Books, 2016) and *The Crafty Poet: A Portable Workshop* (Terrapin Books, revised edition 2016). She has published several full-length collections of poetry, including *The Uneaten Carrots of Atonement* (Wind Publications, 2016); *What Feeds Us,* which received the 2006 Quentin R. Howard Poetry Prize; and *Eve's Red Dress.* Her poems have appeared in such journals as *Beloit Poetry Journal, Southern Poetry Review, Harvard Review, Poet Lore,* and *Prairie Schooner.* In 2015 she founded Terrapin Books, a small press for poetry books, and serves as its editor and publisher.

Alison Luterman is a poet, essayist and playwright. Her books include the poetry collections, *Desire Zoo* (Tia Chucha Press), *The Largest Possible Life* (Cleveland State University Press) and *See How We Almost Fly* (Pearl Editions) and a collection of essays, *Feral City* (SheBooks). Luterman's plays include *Saying Kaddish With My Sister, Hot Water, Glitter and Spew, Oasis,* and *The Recruiter* and the musical, *The Chain.* Her writings have been published in *The Sun, The New York Times, The Boston Phoenix, Rattle, The Brooklyn Review, Oberon, Tattoo Highway, Ping Pong, Kalliope, Poetry East, Poet Lore, Poetry 180, Slipstream,* and other journals and anthologies.

Wesley McNair, who served as Maine's Poet Laureate from 2011-2016, is the author of ten volumes of poetry and two books of nonfiction, and he has edited seven anthologies of Maine writing. The recipient of numerous awards in poetry, McNair has held fellowships from the Fulbright Program, John Simon Guggenheim Memorial Foundation, the National Endowment for the Arts, and the Rockefeller Foundation. He has twice been invited to read his poems by the Library of Congress and was selected for a United States Artists Fellowship as one of America's "finest living artists."

W.S. Merwin was born in New York City in 1927 and was named United States Poet Laureate in 2010. He graduated from Princeton University in 1948, where he studied with John Berryman and R.P. Blackmur. From 1949 to 1951 he worked as a tutor in France, Mallorca, and Portugal; for several years afterward he made the greater part of his living by translating from French, Spanish, Latin, and Portuguese. His first book of poetry, *A Mask for Janus* (1952) was selected by W.H. Auden for the Yale Younger Poets Prize. Since then, Merwin has authored dozens of books of poetry and prose. W.S. Merwin has lived in Hawaii since 1976.

Joseph Millar's first collection, *Overtime,* was a finalist for the 2001 Oregon Book Award. His second collection, *Fortune,* appeared in 2007, followed by a third, *Blue Rust,* in 2012. His latest collection, *Kingdom,* was published in 2017 by Carnegie Mellon. Millar teaches in Pacific University's low-residency MFA Program and in North Carolina State's MFA Program in Creative Writing.

Frederick Morgan (1922-2004) founded *The Hudson Review,* one of the nation's most revered literary journals, and served as its editor for 55 years. He began writing poetry of his own at the age of fifty and published more than a dozen books as well as several anthologies.

Travis Mossotti was awarded the 2011 May Swenson Poetry Award by contest judge Garrison Keillor for his first collection of poems, About the Dead (USU Press, 2011), and his second collection Field Study won the 2013 Melissa Lanitis Gregory Poetry Prize (Bona Fide Books, 2014). His third collection, Narcissus Americana, was selected by Billy Collins as the winner of the 2018 Miller Williams Prize (University of Arkansas Press, 2018). Mossotti teaches in the writing program at Webster University and works for the Office of the Vice Chancellor for Research at Washington University.

Stella Nesanovich is the author of four chapbooks of poems: *A Brightness That Made My Soul Tremble: Poems on the Life of Hildegard of Bingen, My Mother's Breath, My Father's Voice*, and *Dance, O, Heart, Double Round: Poems on Mechthild of Magdeburg* as well as a full-length collection, *Vespers at Mount Angel*. She is Professor Emerita of English at McNeese State University in Lake Charles, Louisiana.

Naomi Shihab Nye describes herself as a "wandering poet." She has spent 40 years traveling the country and the world to lead writing workshops and inspiring students of all ages. Nye was born to a Palestinian father and an American mother and grew up in St. Louis, Jerusalem, and San Antonio. She is the author and/or editor of more than 30 volumes. Her books of poetry include *19 Varieties of Gazelle: Poems of the Middle East*, A Maze Me: Poems for Girls, *Red Suitcase, Words Under the Words, Fuel*, and *You & Yours* (a best-selling poetry book of 2006), and most recently, *The Tiny Journalist* (BOA Editions, 2019).

Alison Prine's poems have appeared or are forthcoming in *Ploughshares, The Virginia Quarterly Review, Shenandoah, Harvard Review, Michigan Quarterly Review*, and *Prairie Schooner*, among others. Her debut collection of poems, *Steel*, was chosen by Jeffrey Harrison for the *Cider Press Review* Book Award and was published in January 2016. *Steel* has been named a finalist for the 2017 Vermont Book Award. Alison Prine lives in Burlington, Vermont where she works as a psychotherapist.

Alberto Ríos was named Arizona's first Poet Laureate in 2013. He is the author of many poetry collections, including *A Small Story About the Sky* (Copper Canyon Press, 2015), *The Dangerous Shirt* (Copper Canyon Press, 2009); *The Theater of Night* (Copper Canyon Press, 2006); and *The Smallest Muscle in the Human Body* (Copper Canyon Press, 2002), which was nominated for the National Book Award.

David Romtvedt is the author of several poetry collections, including *Dilemmas of the Angels* (Louisiana State University Press, 2017); *Some Church* (Milkweed Editions, 2005); *A Flower Whose Name I Do Not Know* (Copper Canyon Press, 1992), chosen by John Haines for the National Poetry Series; and *Moon* (Bieler Press, 1984). Romtvedt served as the poet laureate of Wyoming from 2003 to 2011, and teaches at the University of Wyoming.

Marjorie Saiser is the author of five books of poetry, including *I Have Nothing to Say About Fire* (Backwaters Press, 2016) and co-editor of two anthologies. Her work has been published in *American Life in Poetry, Nimrod, Rattle.com, Poetry Magazine. com, RHINO, Chattahoochee Review, Poetry East, Poet Lore, and other journals.* She has received the WILLA Award and nominations for the Pushcart Prize.

Faith Shearin is the author of five books of poetry: *The Owl Question, The Empty House, Moving the Piano, Telling the Bees,* and *Orpheus Turning.* Recent work has appeared in *Alaska Quarterly Review* and *Poetry East,* and has been read by Garrison Keillor on *The Writer's Almanac.* She is the recipient of awards from The Fine Arts Work Center in Provincetown, The Barbara Deming Memorial Fund, and the National Endowment for the Arts. She lives in West Virginia.

Carrie Shipers is the author of *Ordinary Mourning* (2010), *Cause for Concern* (2015), and *Family Resemblances* (2016). Her poetry has been published in former U.S. Poet Laureate Ted Kooser's column, *American Life in Poetry.* She teaches English and creative writing at Rhode Island College.

Julia Shipley is a poet, author and journalist based in Vermont's Northeast Kingdom. Her work has been featured in *Vermont Life, Orion Magazine,* and *Yankee Magazine,* where she's a contributing editor. Her first book, *The Academy of Hay,* was winner of the Melissa Lanitis Gregory Poetry Prize and a finalist for the 2016 Vermont Book Award. Julia grows fruits and vegetables and raises turkeys and sheep on a six-acre homestead where she lives with her husband and pug.

Anya Silver (1968-2018) won a Guggenheim Fellowship and the Georgia Author of the Year Award. She was the author of four books of poetry, *The Ninety-Third Name of God* (2010), *I Watched You Disappear* (2014), and *From Nothing* (2016), all published by the Louisiana State University Press, as well as *Second Bloom*, which was published in 2017 as part of the Poiema Series of poetry by Cascade Books. Until her death, she taught English at Mercer University in Macon, Georgia.

Tracy K. Smith is the author of the memoir, *Ordinary Light* and four books of poetry: *Wade in the Water* (2018); *Life on Mars*, which received the 2012 Pulitzer Prize; *Duende*, recipient of the 2006 James Laughlin Award; and *The Body's Question*, which won the 2002 Cave Canem Poetry Prize. In 2017 she was named the 22nd U.S. Poet Laureate by the Library of Congress, and was re-appointed to a second term for 2018-19.

Thomas R. Smith is author of seven books of poems, *Keeping the Star* (New Rivers Press, 1988), *Horse of Earth* (Holy Cow! Press, 1994), *The Dark Indigo Current* (Holy Cow! Press, 2000), *Winter Hours* (Red Dragonfly Press, 2005), *Waking Before Dawn* (Red Dragonfly Press, 2007), *The Foot of the Rainbow* (Red Dragonfly Press, 2010), and *The Glory* (Red Dragonfly Press, 2015). He has edited *Walking Swiftly: Writings and Images on the Occasion of Robert Bly's 65th Birthday* (Ally Press, 1992; HarperCollins, 1993) and *What Happened When He Went to the Store for Bread* (Nineties Press, 1993), a selection of the best of the Canadian poet Alden Nowlan, now in its second edition.

Bruce Snider is the author of two poetry collections, *Paradise, Indiana*, winner of the Lena-Miles Wever Todd Poetry Prize, and *The Year We Studied Women*, winner of Felix Pollak Prize in Poetry. He is a former Wallace Stegner fellow and Jones Lecturer at Stanford University, and his poetry and nonfiction have appeared in *American Poetry Review, Poetry, VQR, Iowa Review, Ploughshares, Gettysburg Review, Pleiades, Southern Review* and *Best American Poetry 2012*. He currently teaches at the University of San Francisco.

Kim Stafford is the author of a dozen books of poetry and prose, and the founding director of the Northwest Writing Institute at Lewis & Clark College, where he has taught since 1979. He holds a Ph.D. in Medieval Literature from the University of Oregon, and has worked as a printer, photographer, oral historian, editor, and visiting writer at a host of colleges and schools, and offered writing workshops in Italy, Scotland, and Bhutan. He lives in Portland, Oregon, with his wife and children.

William Stafford's (1914-1993) first collection of poems, *West of Your City*, wasn't published until he was in his mid-forties. However, by the time of his death in 1993, Stafford had published hundreds of poems, and was said to have written at least one new poem a day. His collection, *Traveling Through the Dark*, won the National Book Award for Poetry in 1963. Stafford also received the Award in Literature from the American Academy and Institute of Arts and Letters, a National Endowment for the Arts Senior Fellowship, and the Western States Book Award Lifetime Achievement in Poetry.

Heather Swan's poetry has appeared or is forthcoming in *Poet Lore, The Raleigh Review, Midwestern Gothic, Basalt*, and *Cream City Review*. Her nonfiction has appeared in *Aeon, ISLE, Resilience Journal, About Place,* and *Edge Effects*. Her creative nonfiction book, *Where Honeybees Thrive*, was published by Penn State Press in 2017 and was awarded the Sigurd F. Olson Nature Writing Award. She earned her MFA in poetry and Ph.D. in English and Environmental Studies at University of Wisconsin Madison, where she was also the recipient of the August Derleth Award for Poetry and the Martha Meyer Renk Fellowship in Poetry.

Sam Temple was born and raised in Oregon, and holds an MFA in Creative Writing-Poetry from Eastern Oregon University.

Carmen Tafolla, State Poet Laureate of Texas in 2015 and the first city poet laureate of San Antonio 2012-2014, is the author of more than 30 books, including the latest title in TCU's Poet Laureate Series, *Carmen Tafolla: New and Selected Poems*; *This River Here: Poems of San Antonio*; and the art and poetry collection, *Rebozos,* winner of three International Latino Book Awards. A professor at University of Texas-San Antonio, and President of the Texas Institute of Letters, Tafolla is the recipient of many awards, including the Americas Award, the Charlotte Zolotow, two Tomas Rivera Book Awards, and the Art of Peace Award, for work which contributes to peace, justice and human understanding.

Sue Ellen Thompson is the author of five books of poetry, including her most recent, *THEY* (2014), and her poems have been included in the *Best American Poetry* series, read many times on National Public Radio by Garrison Keillor, and featured in U.S. Poet Laureate Ted Kooser's nationally syndicated newspaper column. Among her awards are the 1986 Samuel French Morse Prize, the 2003 Pablo Neruda Prize, a 2016 Pushcart Prize, and the 2010 Maryland Author Prize from the Maryland Library Association. She lives in Oxford, MD on the Eastern Shore of the Chesapeake, and teaches adult poetry workshops at The Writer's Center in Bethesda.

Natasha Trethewey's first collection of poetry, *Domestic Work* (Graywolf Press, 2000), was selected by Rita Dove as the winner of the inaugural Cave Canem Poetry Prize for the best first book by an African American poet. She is also the author, most recently, of *Monument: Poems New and Selected* (Houghton Mifflin, 2018), which was longlisted for the 2018 National Book Award in Poetry. In 2012, Trethewey was named both the State Poet Laureate of Mississippi and the 19th U.S. Poet Laureate by the Library of Congress. Trethewey is the Board of Trustees Professor of English at Northwestern University in Evanston, Illinois.

Natalia Treviño was born in Mexico City and raised in Texas. She is the author of the poetry collections, *Lavando La Dirty Laundry and VirginX*. She is also a Professor of English at Northwest Vista College and serves on the Advisory Board of the Macondo Writers Workshop. Her poems have won the Alfredo Cisneros de Moral Award, the Wendy Barker Creative Writing Award, the Dorothy Sargent Rosenberg Poetry Prize, the San Antonio Artist Foundation Literary Prize, and the Ditet e Naimet Medana Literary Award in Macedonia.

Connie Wanek is the author of four collections of poetry: *Bonfire* (1997), winner of the New Voices Award from New Rivers Press; *Hartley Field* (2002), *On Speaking Terms* (2010), published by Copper Canyon Press, and *Rival Gardens: New and Selected Poems,* from University of Nebraska Press. She is also co-editor, with Joyce Sutphen and Thom Tammaro, of *To Sing Along the Way: Minnesota Women Poets from Pre-Territorial Days to the Present* (2006). Wanek was named a Witter Bynner Fellow of the Library of Congress by U.S. Poet Laureate Ted Kooser, and in 2009, was named George Morrison Artist of the Year. She lives in New Mexico.

Gillian Wegener is the author of three books of poetry: *Lifting One Foot, Lifting the Other* (In the Grove Press, 2001), *The Opposite of Clairvoyance* (Sixteen Rivers Press, 2008), and her newest collection, *This Sweet Haphazard* (Sixteen Rivers Press, 2017). Her numerous awards for her work include the Dorothy Sargent Rosenberg Poetry Prize in 2006 and 2007, and the Zócalo Public Square Prize for Poetry of Place in 2015. Wegener, a junior high teacher, lives with her husband and daughter in Modesto, where she coordinates and hosts the monthly Second Tuesday Reading Series. She is a cofounder of the Modesto-Stanislaus Poetry Center and has served as the poet laureate for the city of Modesto.

Michelle Wiegers is a contemplative writer who lives in Bennington, Vermont with her husband, children, and many pets. She has published poetry in the *Birchsong Anthology: Volume II* and *Third Wednesday,* among other journals.

Miller Williams (1930-2015) was born in Hoxie, Arkansas and studied at Hendrix College, later earning a master's degree in zoology at the University of Arkansas. He taught at various small colleges until he joined the University of Arkansas English department in 1970. He went on to co-found the University of Arkansas Press, which he directed for two decades, and remained a professor emeritus until his death. Miller was the father of musician Lucinda Williams, and famously read his poem, "Of History and Hope," at President Bill Clinton's second inauguration.

CREDITS

Ellery Akers, "The Word That Is a Prayer," from *Practicing to Tell the Truth*. Copyright © 2015 by Ellery Akers. Reprinted with the permission of Autumn House Press and the author.

Lahab Assef Al-Jundi, "Out of the Mist." Reprinted by permission of author.

David Axelrod, "Mending." Reprinted by permission of author.

William Baer, "Snowflakes," from *Borges and Other Sonnets*. Copyright © 2003 by William Baer. Reprinted with permission of Truman State University Press and author.

Ellen Bass, "Gate C22," from *The Human Line*. Copyright © 2007 by Ellen Bass. Reprinted with the permission of The Permissions Company, Inc. on behalf of Copper Canyon Press, www.coppercanyonpress.org.

Chana Bloch, "Swimming in the Rain," from *Swimming in the Rain: New & Selected Poems*. Copyright © 2015 by Chana Bloch. Reprinted with permission of Autumn House Press.

Megan Buchanan, "My Daughter's Hair," from *Clothesline Religion* Copyright © 2017 by Megan Buchanan. Reprinted with permission of Green Writers Press and author.

with the permission of the University of Arkansas Press, www.uapress. com.

Stella Nesanovich, "Everyday Grace," which first appeared in *Third Wednesday Journal*. Reprinted with permission of the author.

Naomi Shahib Nye, "Shoulders" from *Red Suitcase*. Copyright © 1994 by Naomi Shihab Nye. Reprinted with the permission of The Permissions Company, Inc., on behalf of BOA Editions, Ltd., www. boaeditions.org.

Alison Prine, "Naming the Waves" from *Steel,* Cider Press Review. Copyright © 2016 by Alison Prine. Reprinted with the permission of the author.

Alberto Ríos, "We Are of a Tribe," which also appeared in *Goodbye, Mexico: Poems of Remembrance,* edited by Sarah Cortez, Texas Review Press, 2014. Reprinted with permission of author.

David Romtvedt, "Sunday Morning Early," from *Dilemmas of the Angels,* Louisiana State University Press. © 2017 by David Romtvedt. Reprinted with permission of the author and publisher.

Marjorie Saiser, "For My Daughter" from *I Have Nothing to Say About Fire,* The Backwaters Press. Copyright © 2016 by Marjorie Saiser. Reprinted with permission of the author.

Faith Shearin, "Sight," from *Orpheus, Turning,* Broadkill River Press. Copyright © 2015 by Faith Shearin. Reprinted with permission of the author.

Carrie Shipers, "Mother Talks Back to the Monster," which originally appeared in *North American Review.* Reprinted with permission of the author.

Julia Shipley, "Tokyo, Near Ueno Station," which originally appeared in *Roads Taken: Contemporary Vermont Poetry* edited by Chard deNiord and Sydney Lea, Green Writers Press, 2017. Reprinted with permission of the author.

Anya Silver, "Kindness." Reprinted with permission of the author and Andrew Silver.

Tracy K. Smith, "Beatific" from *Wade in the Water*. Copyright © 2018 by Tracy K. Smith. Reprinted with the permission of The Permissions Company, Inc. on behalf of Graywolf Press, Minneapolis, Minnesota, www.graywolfpress.org.

Thomas R. Smith, "Trust" from *Waking Before Dawn,* Red Dragonfly Press. Copyright © 2007 Thomas R. Smith. Reprinted with permission of the author and publisher.

Bruce Snider, "Forecast" from *Paradise, Indiana*. Pleiades Press. Copyright © 2012 by Bruce Snider. Reprinted with permission of the author and publisher.

Kim Stafford, "Two Arab Men." Reprinted with permission of the author.

William Stafford, "The Way It Is" from *Ask Me: 100 Essential Poems*. Copyright © 1998, 2014 by William Stafford and the Estate of William Stafford. Reprinted with the permission of The Permissions Company, Inc., on behalf of Graywolf Press, Minneapolis, Minnesota, www.graywolfpress.org.

Heather Swan, "Empath." Reprinted with permission of the author.

Carmen Tafolla, "For You I'll Fly." Reprinted with permission of the author.

Sam Temple, "Night Fishing with Poppie." Reprinted with permission of the author.

Sue Ellen Thompson, "Sewing" from *The Golden Hour*. Copyright © 2007 Sue Ellen Thompson. Reprinted with permission of the author and Autumn House Press.

Natasha Trethewey, "Gathering" from *Domestic Work*. Copyright © 1998, 2000 by Natasha Trethewey. Reprinted with the permission of The Permissions Company, Inc., on behalf of Graywolf Press, Minneapolis, Minnesota, www.graywolfpress.org.

Natalia Treviño, "Preserves." Reprinted with permission of the author.

Connie Wanek, "Dowling Gardens," which originally appeared in *upstreet*. Reprinted with permission of the author.

Gillian Wegener, "Letter to My Husband Far Away" from *This Sweet Haphazard*. Copyright © 2017 by Gillian Wegener. Reprinted with permission of the author and Sixteen Rivers Press.

Michelle Wiegers, "With You." Reprinted with permission of the author.

Miller Williams, "Compassion" from *The Ways We Touch: Poems*. Copyright © 1997 by Miller Williams. Used with permission of the University of Illinois Press.

ACKNOWLEDGMENTS

THIS ANTHOLOGY would not exist without the support and encouragement of my husband, Brad Peacock, who pushed me onward every step of the way. Immense thanks to publisher and poet Dede Cummings as well for believing in this book from the very beginning. Ted Kooser's mentorship and friendship over the years have meant more to me than words can ever express, and I especially appreciate his help with this book. I am also indebted to him and his assistant, Pat Hemphill Emile, for their guidance and training during the two years that I worked for *American Life in Poetry* at the University of Nebraska-Lincoln. Many of these poems first appeared in that weekly newspaper column and online at www.americanlifeinpoetry.org. I would not be the poet or editor I am without that valuable editorial experience.

My families, both the Crews and Peacock sides, remind me every day what it means to live from the heart, and I am beyond lucky to be surrounded by so much love and compassion. Boundless gratitude to my community here in Vermont for welcoming me with open arms and giving me a home. There is no better place to be a poet.

Lastly, and most importantly, I am humbled by the generosity of the writers and publishers who allowed me to use their work for this project, in many cases choosing to waive all permission fees. I thank these poets from the bottom of my heart for continuing to write poems that highlight connection at a time when we all sorely need as much kindness as we can get.